COUNSELLING ADULTS WITH LEARNING DISABILITIES

SALLY HODGES

with contributions from NANCY SHEPPARD

Forewords by
SHEILA HOLLINS and VALERIE SINASON

First published 2003 by
PALGRAVE MACMILLAN
Houndmills, Basingstoke, Hampshire RG21 6X5 and 175 Fifth Avenue,
New York, N.Y. 10010
Companies and representatives throughout the world

PALGRAVE MACMILLAN is the global academic imprint of the Palgrave
Macmillan division of St. Martin's Press, LLC and of Palgrave Macmillan
Ltd. Macmillan® is a registered trademark in the United States, United
Kingdom and other countries. Palgrave is a registered trademark in the
European Union and other countries.

ISBN 10:   0–333–96295–8

ISBN 13:   978-0–333–96295–4

1 0 0 5 4 0 9 1 0 8 T

This book is printed on paper suitable for recycling and made from
fully managed and sustained forest sources.

A catalogue record for this book is available from the British Library.

A catalogue record for this book is available from the Library of Congress.
Library of Congress catalogue card number 2002023973.

Printed and bound in Great Britain by
Biddles Ltd, King's Lynn, Norfolk

BASIC TEXTS IN COUNSELLING AND PSYCHOTHERAPY

Series editor: Stephen Frosh

This series introduces readers to the theory and practice of counselling and psychotherapy across a wide range of topic areas. The books appeal to anyone wishing to use counselling and psychotherapeutic skills and are particularly relevant to workers in health, education, social work and related settings. The books are unusual in being rooted in psychodynamic and systemic ideas, yet being written at an accessible, readable and introductory level. Each text offers theoretical background and guidance for practice, with creative use of clinical examples.

Published

Jenny Altschuler
WORKING WITH CHRONIC ILLNESS

Bill Barnes, Sheila Ernst and Keith Hyde
AN INTRODUCTION TO GROUPWORK

Stephen Briggs
WORKING WITH ADOLESCENTS

Alex Coren
SHORT-TERM PSYCHOTHERAPY

Emilia Dowling and Gill Gorell Barnes
WORKING WITH CHILDREN AND PARENTS THROUGH SEPARATION AND DIVORCE

Loretta Franklin
AN INTRODUCTION TO WORKPLACE COUNSELLING

Gill Gorell Barnes
FAMILY THERAPY IN CHANGING TIMES 2nd Edition

Sally Modyes
COUNSELLING ADULTS WITH LEARNING DISABLITIES

Ravi Rana
COUNSELLING STUDENTS

Tricia Scott
INTEGRATIVE PSYCHOTHERAPY IN HEALTHCARE

Geraldine Shipton
WORKING WITH EATING DISORDERS

Laurence Spurling
AN INTRODUCTION TO PSYCHODYNAMIC COUNSELLING

Paul Terry
WORKING WITH THE ELDERLY AND THEIR CARERS

Jan Wiener and Mannie Sher
COUNSELLING AND PSYCHOTHERAPY IN PRIMARY HEALTH CARE

Shula Wilson
COUNSELLING ADULTS WITH LEARNING DISABILITIES

Invitation to authors

The Series Editor welcomes proposals for new books within the Basic Texts in Counselling and Psychotherapy series. These should be sent to Stephen Frosh at the School of Psychology, Birkbeck College, Malet Street, London, WC1E 7HX (e-mail s.frosh@bbk.ac.uk)

Basic Texts in Counselling and Psychotherapy
Series Standing Order ISBN 0–333–69330–2
(outside North America only)

You can receive future titles in this series as they are published by placing a standing order. Please contact your bookseller or, in the case of difficulty, write to us at the address below with your name and address, the title of the series and the ISBN quoted above.

Customer Services Department, Macmillan Distribution Ltd
Houndmills, Basingstoke, Hampshire RG21 6XS, England

CONTENTS

FOREWORD

Sheila Hollins

As Sally Hodges says in page 55, 'counselling is not just about language and words, but about understanding'. The major barrier in the way of competent counselling provision for people with learning disabilities is not the presence of a learning disability, but the lack of understanding of the relevance of counselling by potential referrers. The pathway to specialist help for people with learning disabilities is so often dependent on a third party such as a relative or a paid carer. Few people with learning disabilities refer themselves for counselling or therapy and few counselling services advertise directly to this client group. Sally Hodges has written for a wide range of professionals who work with people with learning disabilities, and introduces theoretical concepts in an accessible way by using clinical vignettes to illustrate each point.

For example, paid carers need to understand how and why their own emotional reactions to the people they support can help them to understand each person better. An introduction to theory and some time spent thinking about different life stages, personal histories, presenting problems and relationship issues will provide an invaluable introduction to the emotional worlds of people with learning disabilities. Many specialist learning disability health and social care professionals have trained in centres where counselling and therapy have not been recognised as valid interventions. Fortunately many such professionals are now seeking post-qualifying courses in counselling or therapy to fill this gap. Mainstream counsellors and therapists whose own training denied them access to people with learning disabilities will welcome the chapters on the historical context, on life stages and relationship issues and on specific presenting problems. The clinical vignettes will bring it to life for them and encourage them to consider a more inclusive approach to service delivery.

How appropriate that a basic textbook on counselling and learning disabilities should emerge from the Tavistock! Pioneering therapeutic work at the Tavistock in the 1980s by Neville Symington, Valerie Sinason and Jon Stokes – among others – paved the way for the present clinical team to develop it further. Much encouraged by colleagues at the Tavistock, Joan Bicknell and I were simultaneously introducing psychodynamic ideas into our developing mental health services for people with learning disabilities in South London. Other psychodynamically orientated psychologists working in the United Kingdom began to evaluate therapy with people with learning disabilities – these were, notably, Nigel Beaill and Pat Frankish, while elsewhere in Europe and the USA similar work was beginning. In May 2000 the Institute of Psychotherapy and Disability was launched at a public meeting at St George's Hospital Medical School, London, attended by nearly 100 interested therapists and professionals. The Institute has started the painstaking work of defining the core competencies of disability psychotherapists. This book will make a significant contribution to these exciting new developments and plans.

SHEILA HOLLINS
Professor of the Psychiatry of Learning Disability
St George's Hospital Medical School
University of London

FOREWORD

Valerie Sinason

In July 2002 Nelson Mandela, the former President of South Africa, made a speech asking fellow-citizens to consider the needs and feelings of those with a learning disability. In the former Czechoslovakia, the first conference on learning disability held after the Russians left was hosted by President Havel and his wife. These national leaders, at times of enormous change, pain and hope, understood how the experience of learning disability had individual, social, spiritual and political dimensions. They also understood how their own formative experiences of being initially in a stigmatised population, deprived of equal rights, allowed them to understand something of the emotional predicament of people with a learning disability.

Indeed, the very history, language, life-stages, relationships and institutional structures of learning disability is filled with human rights issues that are urgently in need of addressing in every country in the world.

Sally Hodges, with Nancy Sheppard as a key contributor, are extremely skilled and empathic practitioners. As counselling psychologists they have written an excellent insightful and practical handbook to help address key issues. The book goes to the psychological heart of disability but does not neglect any of the painful social-interface issues. As an introduction to counselling adults with learning disabilities it offers a thorough discussion of psychoanalytic concepts that aid both the new student and the experienced practitioner. It takes us through the history, the political context, the assessment, life-stages, presenting problems, relationship issues, organisational issues and research and evaluation.

It offers respectful vignettes taken from the lives of clients in treatment or assessment in order to provide aid in thinking about the key issues involved. Chapters have lucid summaries at the end to give the reader a chance to increase the learning potential of their reading.

This book also offers hope for the strengthening and continuing of access to counselling and therapy to those with a learning disability. It will aid psychology, counselling, psychiatry and psychotherapy trainings to increase their provision for this crucial work.

VALERIE SINASON
Consultant Psychotherapist

ACKNOWLEDGEMENTS

Firstly I would like to thank all the clients with whom I have worked, each relationship teaching me something new. Stephen Frosh's editorial feedback has been invaluable and I am very grateful to those who have given me feedback on early drafts of chapters including Rebecca Harris, Kate Stevens, Lynda Miller, Elisa Reyes-Simpson, Maureen Fox and Tony Lee. Alison Caunt and Frances Arnold at Palgrave has been helpful and supportive too. There are so many colleagues, friends, students, and supervisors to whom I feel gratitude for my learning experiences throughout my career, including past and present members of the Tavistock Learning Disabilities Service, the Autism Team and the Child and Family Department at the Tavistock Clinic. I would also like to give my thanks to colleagues in previous departments where I have worked, especially the Redbridge and Plymouth Learning Disabilities Services. On a more personal level, Nige, George and Alfie have all generously tolerated my preoccupation and working absences and for this I thank them.

SALLY HODGES

Nancy Sheppard would like to add the following acknowledgements:

I would like to thank my family for their support and patience over the period of writing my chapters. I am also very grateful to Dr Katrina Scior, Dr Sally Hodges and Dr Harvey Sheppard for their helpful comments in reading early drafts. Finally I would like to acknowledge my clients and colleagues who, over several years, have presented me with a multitude of constructive challenges in my career as a clinical psychologist and provided me with rich and diverse material to draw on to illustrate how helpful counselling and consultation work can be.

NANCY SHEPPARD

INTRODUCTION

Counselling with people with learning difficulties can be the full flowering of human ordinariness. It can help devalued and marginalised people feel much more human, valued and worthwhile, able to cope with the ordinary sufferings and joys of life.
– David Brandon (1989)

Recently I visited a day centre for people with learning disabilities, and was asked to see a young man for counselling. James, I learnt from his keyworker, Sunil, had been given a diagnosis of a terminal brain tumour. Sunil explained that James had come to talk to him in obvious distress wanting to know about the future. Sunil said that he didn't know what to do, he was not a 'trained counsellor', and was not qualified to listen to James. He said 'I'm not a counsellor, I can't talk to him about this.'

It was indeed the case that Sunil had no formal training in counselling, and that James might benefit from some form of therapy. However, James had sought out Sunil as someone who would really listen, think about and try to understand James's experiences.

Sinason (1992) has written about how painful it can be to 'see damage and not be able to repair it, not be able to put it right'. At these times it can be easier not to know, not to be able to respond. Sunil *does* really know how to listen and think about James's distress, even if he is not able to make it better. However, he feels pain and helplessness when James asks him difficult questions and would prefer not to experience these feelings.

The aim of this book is to provide an introduction to psychodynamic and related ideas, both theoretical and practical, about counselling adults with learning disabilities. It is not a training manual for counselling, but rather an introduction to psychodynamic ideas for workers in all caring professions, whose work brings them into contact with people with learning disabilities.

The value of helping people with learning disabilities think about their inner worlds will be explored through case examples. We will also give consideration to the wider systems within which people with learning disabilities function. This means thinking about relationships with families, keyworkers, residential staff and clients, daycentre workers, the local community, as well as wider contexts. I hope to convey my belief in the potential benefits of thinking about peoples' inner worlds, as well as their external realities.

Who might benefit from this book?

It is envisaged that this book might be of use to a range of professionals who work with adults with learning disabilities. It will be of interest to front line workers such as care or residential staff, as well as professionals who have a more directly therapeutic relationship with their clients such as social workers, music, art or movement therapists, counsellors, nurses, psychologists, psychiatrists and psychotherapists. The theory described in this text is mostly psychodynamic theory that relates directly to the field of learning disabilities. Counselling processes that are described will be illustrated with genuine case examples, however all identifying features have been removed or changed, and cases have been amalgamated in order to protect the identity of the people described. My gratitude goes to all the clients with whom I have worked and from whom I have learned.

A note on definitions

Throughout the text the term *people with learning disabilities* will be used. Although a cumbersome term, it is the government recommended term for people with an IQ below the cut-off of 69 (WHO, 1992). Advocacy groups such as People First are clear that this is their preferred term. In this book the clients described fulfil the criteria of having 'learning disabilities' by having an IQ in this range. The learning disabilities range is further divided into Mild (IQ between 55 and 69), Moderate (40–55), Severe (20–40) and Profound (less than 20). It is not necessarily helpful to rely solely on IQ scores when considering a person's functioning for two major reasons. Firstly, emotional difficulties can impact on a person's ability to use their intelligence whatever their IQ score, and secondly, the measurement of IQ is not always accurate for many reasons such as the scope of the testing instruments and the skill of the assessor. These are complicated issues, and in the service where I work, we take into account an individuals' overall functioning, including their adaptive behaviour and emotional state, when thinking about their level of ability.

A note on terminology

Both Sinason (1992) and Marks (2000) have written about the use of language in the field of learning disabilities as a series of shifts in euphemisms. Sinason (1992) points out that no other human group has been forced to change its name so often. She hypothesises that this is related to the painful difference associated with disability and that focusing on the terminology is a way of distancing ourselves from the pain, fear and guilt we cannot change or control. However, the terminology itself quickly becomes an abusive term through the process of distancing, and the term has to be changed once again. Sinason argues that the focus on terminology at worst creates opportunity for abuse (not meeting a person's needs because of following a named strategy such as normalisation in a thoughtless way) and, at best, ignores the rich differences in personality that exist between people whether they have a disability or not.

Structure of the text

The first two chapters will introduce the current contexts for people with learning disabilities, including the social and political contexts, as well as the physical contexts within which they live and function. The main theoretical model used throughout, that of psychodynamic theory, will be described in Chapter 2.

Assessment for counselling is given consideration, both in a formal setting, and also in contexts where formal counselling is not possible, but a questioning frame of mind would be beneficial. A framework for appreciating the impacts of stages in an individual's life span is introduced, and there is a focus on specific 'presenting problems' such as challenging behaviour, abuse and dual diagnosis.

The focus then widens to consider the relationships of people with learning disabilities, their families, friendships, sexual relationships and the benefits of working with groups of people. This section has been written by Nancy Sheppard, a principal clinical psychologist who works with me in the Tavistock Clinic Learning Disabilities Service. This is an all-age service and a more detailed description of the service can be found in Hernandez, Hodges, Miller and Simpson (2000). Both Nancy Sheppard and I have worked in a range of learning disabilities mental health services; between us we have worked for eight different learning disabilities services over eighteen years. This book is the product of our shifting understandings and our belief that people with learning disabilities can benefit from thoughtful counselling. This approach is not dependent on IQ, but more on the emotional understanding that can be co-created, when both the counsellor and the client have the courage to think about and face both painful external realities and the equally painful internal worlds that can exist, colouring how the world may be experienced.

The last chapter considers research and, in particular, the process of evaluating counselling of people with learning disabilities.

1

HISTORICAL CONTEXTS, SETTINGS AND COMMON PRESENTATIONS

In this chapter I consider the political and historical contexts of people with learning disabilities, and the development of a counselling approach to this client group. The historical context is especially important as this group has traditionally been devalued, and the way in which it is viewed has important implications for the development of a therapeutic relationship with each individual client. Various contexts within which adults with learning disabilities live, work and spend their time are described, with particular emphasis on the way in which psychological distress may be manifest and recognised. These are all contexts within which a counselling approach can be utilised.

Historical approaches to people with learning disabilities

When considering a person's inner world it is important to be mindful about not only their personal history, but also their culture and the history of the groups to which they belong. When working with children of refugees or victims of torture or racism, it makes no sense to ignore how their predecessors have been treated and viewed. The past treatment of ancestors becomes integrated into families and individuals as folklore, religion, customs or accepted ways of being. This is also true of people with learning disabilities, although, just as with other minority groupings, there is a tendency to ignore or minimise the impact of the past (Atkinson *et al.*, 1997). Brendon McCormack (1991) has described how a learning disability can be thought of as a communication difficulty in three areas: with others, oneself (thinking) and one's background or history. He points out that removing people from their homes and communities, as has been the policy over the last century, is an active removal from their historical contexts. More often than not, a person's history is not communicated to staff when they move, and files can be painfully thin for the experiences of a person's lifetime. This can negate the meanings of these experiences and the dynamic nature of experience and ability to think, or to use one's intelligence; this idea will be discussed more fully later.

Documented approaches

Early records dating back to ancient Greek and Roman times indicate that infanticide was practised on sick or deformed children (Barnes, 1994). Cruelty and mistreatment of people with learning disabilities have been documented as occurring over the centuries since then. Before the nineteenth century, the evidence available for understanding how people with learning disabilities were conceptualised tends to be laws or legal documents. Such documentation makes it hard to gain an understanding of how people with learning difficulties were thought about, what their lives would have been like, where they lived and how they were treated.

We know that during the period between medieval times and the nineteenth century there were no specific laws or guidance for treatment of people with learning disabilities, and this lack of focus has led historians to classify these times as either a 'golden age' or an 'era of neglect' (Caine *et al.*, 1998). During these times people were classified by law as either 'lunatics' (acquired and punctuated by times of lucidity) or 'idiots' (present from birth and constant) (Andrews, 1996). However people only tended to get a label of idiot if they came to the attention of the courts or poor law administrators, either through financial difficulties or extremes of behaviour.

There was a noticeable shift in treatment of people with learning disabilities at the end of the nineteenth century, when Victorian ideas about the importance of education seemed to influence policy makers. There are debates in the literature as to what exactly the precipitating factors were (Wright, 1996), but the outcome was clear; people with learning disabilities were institutionalised on a large scale. The urbanisation that occurred in the Victorian era increased the visibility of people with learning disabilities, and this led to the perception of people with learning disabilities as a social problem. The major reasons parents gave for having their children institutionalised were on the grounds of poor educational performance.

The shift in how people with learning disabilities were conceptualised was significant, and Locke's distinction between madness (right reasoning from wrong principles) and idiocy (lack of reasoning ability) was adopted. Caine et al. (1998) point out that as reasoning ability was considered a defining characteristic of humanity, 'idiots' were considered less than human, lacking in intelligence and qualitatively different from other people (ideas which they point out still persevere today).

Although many of the large institutions were developed with the notion of being a short-term educational facility, with the aims of training 'idiots' to become productive members of society, for economic reasons incarceration developed into a lifelong sentence.

The next major change in the conceptualisation of learning disabilities occurred around the end of the nineteenth century. People with learning disabilities started to be seen as a threat to society. This seemed to be linked to the development of the medical profession who saw idiocy as an organic and perhaps inheritable disease, which required medical treatment. Dale (1995) describes how whole families could feel guilt and blame as a family with a learning disabled member became viewed as a 'sick' or pathological family.

Further, as the eugenics movement gained momentum, there was a growing concern that social problems were being created by the reproduction of poor genetic stock. Human traits were viewed as heritable, so the next logical step was to claim that 'idiots' should be prevented from having children.

CASE EXAMPLE: Gladys

About ten years ago, I was asked to see an elderly lady who was being assessed for a move from a long stay mental handicap hospital into the community. The hospital staff were concerned that she had become very withdrawn and depressed, refusing to talk to the staff and curling up and crying for her mother. Her file was requested, and this took some time to arrive, as it was kept in the basement storage system of the hospital (meaning that none of her current care staff had any idea about her background or history). When it arrived, I was very shocked to see that the reason for Gladys's admission, sixty-five years previously, was for having had an illegitimate child, a daughter, when she was thirteen. There was no documentation about learning disabilities at all. I wondered about the possible meaning of having to leave her lifetime home, not only the loss of the familiar environment, but also the memory of her child, and her previous life. It raised questions about how she felt about the difficult separation from her child. It was then possible to think about the importance of talking with Gladys about her history, and reflecting with the staff about the importance of seeing her as a person with a valuable and relevant past. This awareness might bring anxiety and pain, but for Gladys it seemed to enable her to make sense of what she was feeling at this difficult time of transition. Sadly, such backgrounds are not uncommon, and as a result the relevance of peoples' life experiences is frequently minimised.

The development of the profession of psychology added weight to the process of segregation. Possibly in common with the medical profession's emphasis on diagnosis, psychologists and educationalists worked on refining IQ tests as a way of classifying people, basing segregation on a person's score on the test. The development of the terms 'imbecile' and 'feeble-minded' and, most importantly, 'moral imbecility' can be connected with this development. It became seen as more acceptable to incarcerate people for their behaviour, owing to the umbrella definition of 'mental deficiency' (Jackson, 1996).

The Welfare State

In 1948 the National Health Service was created and, in conjunction with Social Services, it still organises the bulk of service provision to people with learning disabilities. As the large-scale institutions fell under the administration of the NHS, there was a gradual but definite shift of emphasis in care: 'inmates' became 'patients' with health care needs.

This redefinition allowed for a shift in the perception of people with learning disabilities, the emphasis on them as a threat to society was reduced, and this allowed for a new perception to develop. For example, the civil rights of people with learning disabilities began to be questioned. In the 1970s the work of Wolfensburger highlighted the shortfalls in society that prevented people with learning disabilities having access to normal activities and services (Wolfensberger, 1972). Other factors contributing towards the most recent shifts included research evidence suggesting that skills teaching and education could be of use to people previously considered 'ineducatable'.

These changes, combined with the public scandals of mistreatment of patients within the larger institutions (Mittler and Sinason, 1996), led to the 1971 White Paper 'Better Services for the Mentally Handicapped', which strongly recommended increasing 'community care'. The emphasis of care had once again shifted from health to social needs.

Current social and political contexts

'The National Health Service and Community Care Act' 1990, came into effect in 1993. This paper promoted the services that would enable people with learning disabilities to live in their own homes. It was envisaged that people would live in local communities so that the large long stay hospitals could be gradually and completely closed down, a process which is almost entirely complete in the UK.

With housing and social needs addressed, attention has shifted to the mental health needs of people with learning disabilities. There is debate across the country as to where best these needs should be met; should services be attached to adult mental health services, or better placed within social services, or even exist in their own right? This debate seems to reflect a wider cultural difficulty in thinking about the needs of people with learning disabilities, and the difficulty in recognising that the group itself is not homogeneous. Delays and lack of clarity in service provision can have serious implications, given the very high incidence of mental health problems for people with learning disabilities.

The power of images and representation in the media

Deborah Marks (2000) has explored in detail the impact language, images and representations in the media and western society have on people with disabilities. For example, people with disabilities are frequently portrayed in films as isolated and excluded, whereas intelligence is equated with beauty and fitness. Although it can often be the case that people with disabilities are isolated and lonely, this can only be perpetuated by the way in which disability is publicised or represented. Marks notes how disability is never presented as incidental, but is always a central topic, and that disability on television is not representative of the incidence of disability within the population. Disability is over-represented as the focus of films, but under-represented on television, for example in soap operas. Marks also explores how disabled people in films are almost always represented by 'non disabled' adults (though one could question how obtainable equity cards, the unit of qualification in acting, are to people with disabilities). She argues that the core of the difficulty in representing disability in the media is that it allows the observer the luxury of thinking that 'it's not real, it's only pretend'. This has the effect of making viewers feel once removed from the reality of disability, and the fear, fantasies of loss or dependence can be more safely experienced or explored. By representing disabled people as objects of pity, it allows us to split off and project into these images our own disabilities and weaknesses. Hostile feelings are quickly transformed into feelings of guilt or pity.

Another major source of imagery regarding disabilities is the media. Here, too, disability is depicted in a certain way, as something to be avoided and overcome. One frequent example is that of Down's syndrome. Recently there has been great media interest in new developments in Japan where it has been identified that Down's Syndrome can be identified through a maternal blood test, reducing the necessity for intrusive assessments such as amniocentesis. The implication is that it enables parents to make a choice earlier if they wish to abort the 'disabled' foetus. People with genetic syndromes are confronted with such negative messages on a regular basis. As Sinason (1992) reflected, there is a fine line between 'you should not have been born' (we are going to prevent people like you being born) and 'you should be dead'. For people with learning disabilities this focus on how to prevent disabilities in infants, as well as the drive to cure disabilities through medicine, gives a powerful message to them that they are unwanted, which can lead to an internalised sense that people would prefer it if they disappeared or died.

The importance of highlighting these issues is not to criticise the way disability is represented in western society, but to raise awareness of these issues. When working with people with disabilities, it is important to be aware of the impact of the many experiences they have on a daily basis. It is also important to be aware of one's own thoughts, beliefs and experiences of disability, and the impact that images and representations can have on one's own functioning.

Developments in theoretical approaches

There is a consensus in the literature that the field of learning disabilities is shifting. For the majority of the twentieth century it was considered that talking treatments were not appropriate for people with learning disabilities. This situation has been traced back to a comment made by Freud (1905) that a certain degree of verbal ability was required for psychoanalysis. Freud aired this view at a critical time, when the ideas about talking treatments were only just starting to catch public interest. The effect of this early comment has been long-lasting and although there have been pockets of psychodynamic work with people with learning disabilities (for example, Clark, 1933; Mannoni, 1968) it was not really until the early 1980s that a consistent body of literature developed in which a 'talking' treatment was promoted. In the meantime the behavioural work originating in the 1920s and 1930s retained a firm grip on the field of learning disabilities for a number of reasons. The use of behavioural work has arguably been popular because behavioural methods have been perceived as more testable and therefore 'scientific'; they enabled efficacy to be researched and produced results that gave numerical outcome data. Behavioural methods also allowed for a distancing from the person; professionals were not required to get to know clients or to interact with them, and this provided a solution for avoiding the fear of and guilt associated with disability.

The development in 'talking treatments' with people with learning disabilities, or perhaps the reduction in 'therapeutic disdain' (Bender, 1993) probably came about for a number of reasons, including the climate change towards people with learning disabilities described above. There was also a considerable shift in policy development in the late seventies and early eighties towards people with learning disabilities. For example, the 1971 Education Act stated very clearly that no child is 'ineducable' and that services to children need to adapt in order to provide the most constructive learning environment. Other important developments include Wolfensberger's (1972) work on Normalisation, and the development of important advocacy groups such as People First. These groups, some of which were staffed entirely by people with learning disabilities, pushed the way forward for equality and supported their members in accessing mainstream mental health services.

Who might benefit from a counselling approach? Settings and presenting problems

'Talking' treatments are now being considered viable in a large range of settings. The range of settings where people with learning disabilities live, work or spend their time is now wide.

Case examples will illustrate some possibilities of where people might be living or spending their time; through these, common presenting problems will also be illustrated, although these examples are by no means exhaustive of either problems or settings.

CASE EXAMPLE: Group Homes

Lorraine is a twenty-two year old woman who has mild learning disabilities. She lives in a group home, which is managed by the health service and has seven residents. The home had been created by knocking together two terraced houses in a residential street. From the outside it would not be possible to tell that this is a facility for people with learning disabilities; there are no obvious signs. The home is staffed by a core group of ten care staff, who work on a rota basis, two or three are on duty during the day, and one staff member sleeps in overnight. On the whole, the residents are quite cognitively able though all have a learning disability. Each resident is assigned a keyworker, and Lorraine's keyworker, Debbie, is becoming concerned that Lorraine has been going out without saying where she is going, and coming back quite late at night. Also, a small sum of money has gone missing from one of the residents rooms, and when the staff team asked the group about this, Lorraine became very angry, saying that she was being accused. She then ran out of the house, not returning until late, again refusing to tell anyone where she had been. Debbie found a time when Lorraine was a little calmer, and instead of asking her questions about where she had been and what she had been doing, Debbie talked to Lorraine about how she thought Lorraine might be feeling: perhaps lonely and cross that staff were not very good at taking notice of her unless she behaved in a way they found difficult. Lorraine burst into tears and said she did want to talk to someone, but not Debbie, not someone from the home. Debbie suggested a referral for counselling, which Lorraine agreed to.

CASE EXAMPLE: Hostels

Ms McDougall is a twenty-nine-year-old woman who is living in a temporary hostel for women with learning disabilities. She has moderate learning disabilities, and a slight weakness on her left side, which makes her uneven on her feet.

The hostel has five rooms and is run by social services. Residents are moved in as an emergency measure, because it has been judged that their safety cannot be guaranteed in their current placement. It is, however, considered to be a temporary placement and there is the expectation that residents will not stay much longer than two years at the most. For this reason, the rooms are rather stark and impersonal though there is a welcoming communal area. There is a twelve person staff team who work on a rota basis where there are always at least two staff on duty at any time, nights included. Ms McDougall was given a place at the hostel when she disclosed that her stepfather had been sexually abusing her. She disclosed the abuse to her social worker, who had been concerned about Ms McDougall's behaviour when taken swimming as a supported day activity; she had refused to get undressed and had been very tearful. Her mother refused to believe that she was being abused, and is still very angry about her accusations. Criminal prosecution procedures were taken against her stepfather, but the CPS felt that because of Ms McDougall's learning disability the case would not be successful so it was not taken to court.

Ms McDougall had been living in the hostel for eighteen months and staff were preparing her for a move into the community; recently, however, a number of concerns about Ms McDougall's behaviour have developed. She has been smearing her faeces and masturbating openly in the communal areas. The staff team agreed that one of the hostel staff, Naomi, would make time to talk to Ms McDougall to try and understand her behaviour.

Ms McDougall was initially very angry towards Naomi, shouting and swearing, saying 'what do you care, you just want to get rid of me'. Naomi was able to make helpful links to Ms McDougall about how she was feeling 'got rid of' by the hostel now, and how she felt 'got rid of' by her mother and stepfather, when she told what had been happening. It was then possible for Naomi to reflect with Ms McDougall about how she had found it difficult to talk about her feelings, linking this with the response on disclosure of the abuse: rejection and disbelief.

CASE EXAMPLE: Supported Living

Mr Michaels is in his forties and is wheelchair-bound. He has cerebral palsy and mild learning disabilities. He lived with his parents until their deaths when he was in his late thirties. Throughout his life he has had carers come into his family home to help with washing and dressing, increasingly so as his parents became less able. Following their deaths within two years of each other, Mr Michaels developed severe depression. He was unable to stay living in the family home for financial reasons, and he was offered the possibility of moving in to a group home for adults with learning disabilities. He declined this offer saying that they were all 'mentally disabled' not like himself. He was then offered a supported living situation, where he was given a ground floor flat to live in on his own with support staff organised to visit on a daily basis to help him with daily living tasks. Mr Michaels appreciates his independence, though he is lonely, and this seems to be contributing towards his depression. His social worker, Miles, has noticed how withdrawn he has become, and how he shows reluctance to go to the local adult training centre drop-in, where he was a keen attendee. Miles suggested that they took some time to talk about his feelings and Mr Michaels agreed.

CASE EXAMPLE: Independent Living

Mr and Mrs Hart both have mild learning disabilities, and are in their twenties, having been married for two years. Their marriage was arranged by their very supportive families, who have provided them with a home to live in. Neither Mr or Mrs Hart are employed, they each get disability living allowances. They have a mutually supportive relationship, Mr Hart does most of the cooking and shopping, as Mrs Hart has a slight physical disability that makes walking long distances difficult for her, and she does the cleaning and washing, which she undertakes with great pride. The couple have a social worker, Eleanor, who visits them every three or four months. On her most recent visit, she found the couple had been arguing, and the state of the house was deteriorating. Both Mr and Mrs Hart seemed quite angry with each other, but seemed unable to listen to each other's point of view. They objected to Eleanor trying to help, saying it was none of her business, and so she suggested that they see someone independently to talk through their worries. They refused this, but two weeks after this visit Mr Hart telephoned Eleanor to say that things had got worse, Mrs Hart had gone back to live with her parents, but she was agreeing to talk with him if someone else was there. Eleanor referred the couple for counselling.

There are a range of other possible settings in which people with learning disabilities can live. These include residential or village type communities, which consist of groups of homes which tend to be run by social or voluntary organisations and often have a strong philosophical or religious orientation. Since the 1990 Community Care Act, people with learning disabilities are more likely to be living as adults in their families of origin, as there are fewer community placements available.

There are a wide range of day services that people with learning disabilities can have access to, in common with the non-disabled population, such as employment, work clubs, social clubs, health-based centres, cinemas and other entertainment centres. Staff in day centres may often be called upon to provide a supportive, counselling or psychotherapeutic relationship. The range of day activities is explored through the use of case examples.

CASE EXAMPLE: Day Centres

Elizabeth is a twenty-one year old woman with Down's syndrome who lives at home with her parents, her younger brother and her older sister. Four days a week she attends the local day centre for people with learning disabilities, where she has a timetable of arranged activities. The centre is a modern purpose-built building, which is cheerfully decorated and is set on a landscaped plot of land, hidden behind a row of trees. Elizabeth is learning catering skills and computer skills and she attends a social skills group. Elizabeth is collected by local authority transport to attend the centre, and she often goes out on supervised weekend or evening trips with the centre staff and attendees. Over the last few months, staff have noticed that Elizabeth has become more withdrawn. She did not attend out of hours activities for several weeks and even more recently has not turned up to the centre. She also got into an argument with another client, which seemed most out of character.

One of the staff members, Mrs Sharp, has always been quite fond of Elizabeth, and decided to try and talk to Elizabeth about her concerns. Elizabeth was sullen and said that nothing was wrong. Mrs Sharp asked Elizabeth's parents to come in for a review, which Elizabeth attended. Her parents said that they had not noticed any change in Elizabeth recently, but thought that she was probably caught up in the excitement of her sister's forthcoming wedding, on which the whole family were very focused. As Elizabeth's mother talked about this, Elizabeth looked very distressed, and Mrs Sharp had the feeling that Elizabeth was holding back tears. Later, after this meeting, when Mrs Sharp spoke gently to Elizabeth about how she might be feeling that her sister was getting married and leaving home, Elizabeth sobbed, and Mrs Sharp was then able to talk to her about a referral for counselling which Elizabeth welcomed.

CASE EXAMPLE: Flexible day support

Mr Hastings is a thirty-year old man, who lives in a group home with three other men. He has a learning disability, and is the most able of the residents of his group home. There is no suitable adult training centre in his locality, so a day programme has been created to best suit his needs. He attends a work experience centre one day a week, he has a part-time job in a factory two days a week and he goes out on regular day trips with a group of people with mild learning disabilities one day every other week.

Recently he was arrested for exposing himself in the local park to a group of children, and it transpired that he had kept a collection of child pornography at home. The police decided not to prosecute him as it was a first offence and he has a disability. Instead, they recommended a referral for counselling for Mr Hastings. Mr Hasting's GP has referred him to his local adult learning disability team, which consists of a psychiatrist, psychologists, nurses and counsellors.

CASE EXAMPLE: Work experience centres

Carlos is a nineteen-year old man with a mild learning disability. He lives at home with his elderly parents. His four brothers and sisters have all moved out over the last fifteen years, and he has been on his own at home for the last three years. He finished school for people with mild to moderate disabilities in August and for the last four months he has been attending a work experience centre on a daily basis. The centre is primarily set up to teach carpentry and gardening skills to people with mild learning disabilities. They have several contracts with local garden centres to provide garden woodwork such as furniture and fences. The attendees get paid a wage for attending the centre, out of the profits. Staff have noticed that Carlos refuses to work alongside employees who have an obvious physical disability, and that he uses racist language. He has been appointed a key worker, Mick, who has the task of trying to talk to Carlos about this behaviour. His task is twofold and thus complicated: he has to let Carlos know that this behaviour will not be tolerated, as well as trying to understand Carlos' difficult behaviour.

CASE EXAMPLE: Further education

Ms Caine is a thirty-two year old woman with a moderate learning disability. Since leaving school ten years ago she has attended an adult day centre, but at a review two years ago, she said that she would like to develop her literacy skills. The following academic year she was offered a place at the local FE college on a course designed for people with learning disabilities. This college is a large purpose built building which caters for people with and without disabilities, from eighteen upwards. It runs a range of academic and skills-based courses, many of which lead to a qualification such as the NVQ.

Ms Caine attends the college one day a week, and over the last week there have been growing concerns about her aggressive behaviour. She has hit out at other students, once stabbing a student in the hand with her pen. She can be verbally aggressive and rude to staff at the college. She lives at home with her mother (her father died recently) and her mother has been called in to a review with the course tutor and head in the next month.

There are many relationships that people with learning disabilities may develop that provide settings for counselling. These include advocacy services, befriending services, social services, religious based services and consumer led services such as People First. People with learning disabilities may be more likely to talk to, or express their feelings to, the people they feel closest to; sometimes, however, it can be easier to talk when the recipient will not be seen on a regular basis. Sometimes it can be very difficult to provide regular private time, but this does not mean that boundaries such as privacy should be ignored, as can frequently happen for people with learning disabilities. This issue needs to be worked out on an individual basis. However, it is our responsibility to think about, and recognise, when the people we work with, perhaps on a daily basis, become distressed or disturbed.

SUMMARY

- Historically people with learning disabilities have been devalued and misunderstood. This historical legacy can have an ongoing impact with every new encounter a person with learning disabilities makes.
- On a societal level, devalued groups tend to attract further devaluation, as it can be easier to create a sense of a 'them and us' distinction or split, the devalued group then attracting all the negative attributes and shortcomings felt by others. One such example is the once pervasive idea that people with learning disabilities 'do not have the same kind of feelings' as 'normal' people so there is no point in talking with them.
- On a personal or one-to-one level, the process of internally splitting between attributes that are valued and those which are not, then pushing out the aspects of ourselves which are less valued on to those who are more obviously damaged is a subtle and normally unrecognised process that can hinder development both in individuals and within families.
- People with learning disabilities have been much overlooked for counselling treatments, though gradually and surely there has been a shift. There is a growing awareness of the mental health needs of people with learning disabilities, and of the utility of counselling approaches.
- People with learning disabilities live and spend their time in a wide range of different settings, and they are likely to come into contact with a range of many different professionals throughout their lifetime. It is all of our responsibilities to ensure that when needed they have access to equitable mental health services, and to provide a thoughtful approach that facilitates access to such services.
- When a counselling approach is used with a person with learning disabilities, it should be afforded with respect. This means providing private space to talk, as well as consistent and predictable boundaries around what is said.

2

THEORETICAL DEVELOPMENTS

There are three core aspects to the psychodynamic model of counselling. Firstly, we all have aspects of our functioning that we do not have direct access to, parts that we may not understand and that can influence how we feel and behave. These areas of functioning are called the *unconscious*. A belief in the importance and significance of the unconscious is what makes psychodynamic counselling different from other kinds of talking treatments such as supportive or cognitive therapy. The second aspect is that the unconscious can find a way of expressing itself through the processes of *transference* and *countertransference*. Transferences are the processes whereby feelings in the client related to past experiences which have become unconscious are transferred onto the relationship with the counsellor. That is, feelings are drawn into the therapeutic relationship that have a source elsewhere. Countertransferences are the feelings and experiences that are evoked in the counsellor that specifically relate to the relationship with the client. The third aspect to the model is that we all develop a range of *defences* in order to keep us from developing a more conscious awareness of what our unconscious contains. These ideas will be further explained and illustrated with case examples, starting with the idea of the unconscious.

The unconscious

The term *psychodynamic* refers to active unconscious processes within the psyche, or to the fluidity between what is conscious and what is unconscious within a person's mind. The aim of psychodynamic counselling is to enable the movement of these feelings into greater consciousness, and in the process, to alleviate some of the distress that is associated with any such unresolved feelings. It is assumed in this model that when a person presents with psychological difficulties, there must be some degree of unresolved, unconscious conflict, and that the person could benefit from the process of understanding these conflicts. Melanie Klein's work has helped enormously in our understanding of the nature of a person's unconscious world and how it is formed through our very early relationships. Before we think about Klein's work, we will consider Freud's role in shaping psychodynamic theory.

The beginning of a psychodynamic approach

Just over a hundred years ago, Sigmund Freud, a doctor, became curious about the hysterical nature of some of his adult patients' physical symptoms and he started to experiment with treatments that involved talking, as opposed to physical or medical interventions. He hypothesised that these patients' difficulties were being expressed through physical symptoms, but had their root in conflicts that the patients could not directly recognise or understand, that is, *unconscious conflict*. Freud initially used the term 'talking cure' for his methods, then later developed the term 'psychoanalysis' to describe this treatment (Freud, 1910). Freud stated that 'a certain measure of natural intelligence and ethical development are to be required' for his methods (Freud, 1904). He wasn't ruling out psychotherapy for people with learning disabilities, but he thought his methods would need alteration for this client group.

Freud (1912) was the first to describe the processes of *transference* and *countertransference* within a therapeutic relationship. Although our understanding of both processes has developed since Freud's original work, (for example, through the work of Heimann, 1950, and Money-Kyrle, 1956) transferences are still considered to be core processes to any psychotherapeutic relationship, and to making sense of the clients' psychological symptoms.

Although both transference and countertransference are accepted as central aspects of counselling relationships, the emphasis upon these processes in counselling people with learning disabilities could be considered as slightly different; 'normal' adults tend to have access to a greater range of vocabulary, and may be more able to verbally communicate their experiences and transferences to the counsellor. For this reason the process of transference, the unconscious, and often wordless, communication of feelings, can take on greater significance in the counselling relationship with a client with learning disabilities. This significance is similar to contemporary child psychotherapy, where all aspects of communication are closely attended to. So play, use of eye contact, looking, drawing, body movements and tones of voice can all be important sources of information about the relationship created with the client, and therefore provide information about the client's inner world.

Countertransference

CASE EXAMPLE: Denise

Jane works as a residential social worker in a home for seven learning disabled residents. She is a keyworker to Denise who has mild learning disabilities. Jane recently noticed that whenever she spends a significant amount of time with Denise, she ends up with uncomfortable feelings of frustration, anger and sadness. Jane organised a consultation meeting with me, in my role as a consultant to the staff group. She described how Denise has been a cause for concern for several months now, as she has seemed to be very angry with everyone she interacts with. Denise always seems to talk as if she has nothing to worry about and denies ever feeling any upset or distress. She often says 'leave me alone, I don't want or need your help' to the staff. In our meeting Jane talked about her curiosity about these feelings of sadness that Denise seems to elicit in her. Jane then spontaneously started to talk about Denise's early life. Denise's mother was a chronic drug addict. She could not cope with any of her six children, often leaving them to fend for themselves and she physically abused Denise on many

Continued

occasions. There is no mention in the notes of Denise's father; it is apparent that very little is known about him. Denise, with her brothers and sisters, was placed in care on a number of occasions throughout her childhood. Denise was placed in foster care for eight months when she was just six months old, as her mother was having real difficulties in coping. As Jane talked about Denise's distressing and neglected childhood, she started to make some links between Denise's difficult behaviour and Denise's mother's erratic and absent behaviour. For example she wondered if Denise pushed other people away as it reflected her experience of being pushed away herself.

Jane then talked about the current plans to organise independent living for Denise. She is more able than the other residents in the home, and the staff feel convinced that she could cope with her own place. This plan is in line with the local authority's policy on promoting independent living, and Denise's social worker also has hopes that this will boost her self confidence. As Jane described these plans, she said with some recognition, 'Really it's a lot for her to cope with, and she will lose us; perhaps Denise has been affected by all the plans. I have been too annoyed with her behaviour to think about what she might be feeling like'.

Following our meeting, Jane organised some time to talk with Denise when they would not be disturbed. During this meeting, instead of asking Denise questions about why she was behaving in a certain way, Jane encouraged Denise to talk about her worries, and then Jane was able to reflect on some of the links between Denise's behaviour and perhaps her less conscious feelings about loss. Denise looked relieved, and instead of getting angry, she started to cry.

This example illustrates several important aspects of creating a relationship that aims to be therapeutic. These are:

- the understanding that behaviour always has meaning
- the belief that one's early life experiences have lasting effects
- the awareness that being open to one's own feelings and responses is an essential part of providing counselling.

Jane was able to think about possible meanings behind Denise's behaviour; she had made sure to inform herself about Denise's history and most importantly she was open and sensitive to the feelings Denise generated in her. This meant thinking about all of her feelings and making a distinction about which were generated from within her, and which originated from her relationship with Denise. This skill is an essential aspect of providing psychotherapeutic counselling to people with learning disabilities. Jane was open enough to allow herself to experience (to make conscious) some of what Denise might be feeling. In psychodynamic terms this is referred to as *countertransference*. Countertransferance is our conscious and unconscious reactions and responses to another person, and it is important to be aware of this process in working with people with learning disabilities. This is because they are less likely to be able either to identify or to verbally express their feelings owing to cognitive, language or emotional difficulties or, more often than not, a combination of all three of these. A common countertransference response when working with people with learning disabilities is that of time passing very slowly or of overwhelming tiredness and an urge to go to sleep. This response is more common with this client group because of the increased likelihood of very painful feelings and experiences being evoked, and can be thought about as a reaction to the presence of something overwhelmingly difficult to think about. Our responses can help us to identify which aspects of being with a client are more difficult; and being thoughtful and sensitive to these responses is the start of the process of trying to make some sense of the client's inner world.

When Freud first described countertransference, he saw it as a hindrance to his work, because he felt his own feelings were interfering with his understanding of his patient's feelings. However, the fact that he did identify that it was occurring, and that he gave voice to it, was a critical development in our understanding of people's inner worlds. It was not until the work of Heimann (1950) and Bion (1959) that its application was more fully appreciated. Heimann (1950) pointed out that countertransference is a specific response to the client, not just the counsellor's own unhelpful feelings. Bion (1959), using the idea of countertransference and more specifically the idea of *projective identification*, described one aspect of the unconscious process between very young infants and their carers in his development of the concept of *maternal containment* described below.

To some extent we all rely on countertransference in our daily lives. As a skill it can help us understand other peoples' feelings and internal conflicts, by noticing and thinking about how they make us feel.

Alvarez and Reid (1999) describe the use of countertransference when working with people with autism. They illustrate how important using one's responses to the client is in counselling, especially when the client is less verbal or very stuck in their symptoms. They make the point that people with autism do not evoke the same kinds of feelings in the workers, because a core aspect of their difficulties is with a 'lack of feeling', so the counsellor has to work very hard at reclaiming their interest (Alvarez, 1992) and 'demonstrating' that the world beyond their difficulties is indeed interesting (Reid, 1988). Using countertransference enables the counsellor to recognise and observe how tiny changes in their behaviour may trigger changes in the client that can be used to engage the client: 'the therapist must have a mind for two, energy for two, hope for two, imagination for two. Gradually patients may begin to get interested, not yet in us, but in our interest in them' (Alvarez and Reid, 1999, p. 7). Much of this understanding is relevant to working with adults with learning disabilities, particularly those with severe and profound disabilities, who, like people with autism, may have a limited repertoire of expression.

Using countertransference responses when working with people with learning disabilities is an essential skill. Not only are people disadvantaged verbally through cognitive impairment, they are also likely to be disadvantaged by the lack of encouragement to express their feelings. Although the ability to recognise emotional responses to other people is an important skill in counselling people with learning disabilities, it cannot be used effectively if the counsellor is not able to think about his or her own feelings, motivations and prejudices. Supervision and indeed personal therapy can make an essential difference in understanding the very complex emotional relationships created through our clinical work. This is why in the training of professionals who rely heavily on the use of transference and countertransference in their work, there is a requirement and a commitment to undergo personal analysis. For all professionals whose aim is to alleviate distress through interpersonal relationships, an opportunity to think about their own emotional inner worlds is a very helpful and necessary process.

Transference

In considering the process of transference we will return to Denise, who was introduced earlier in this chapter.

CASE EXAMPLE: Denise

In Denise's last individual review, her social worker and the home manager talked about starting the process of organising an independent living placement for Denise. A local housing association had built a set of self contained flats designed specifically for people with disabilities. Denise was very excited about this proposal, she said she was 'not disabled like them others' (residents in her home), and she couldn't wait to get away. Denise's positive response and excellent behaviour resulted in the plans for her independent placement to be moved forward quickly. However, over the last few months Denise has been increasingly sullen and rude to Jane, her key-worker, and the other staff and residents at her home. She has lost her temper for no clear reason, and very recently she tried to hit Jane, which surprised everyone as Denise has always been quite fond of Jane. Initially, Jane described to me how she feels like giving up on Denise, 'the sooner we organise her placement the better, it's what she wants after all, and I don't see why I should have to put up with all her aggression'.

As we discussed Denise's history, some of her behaviour started to make more sense. Denise has been neglected, abused and abandoned on many occasions throughout her childhood, from when she was a very young baby. Although she says she is keen to move, it is as if unconsciously she is pushing the staff to get rid of her quickly. It seems as if Denise is recreating the difficult relationship she had with her mother, with the home staff and especially with Jane.

This process is called *transference*. Freud (1912) described transference as occurring when psychological experiences are revived, and instead of being located in the past, they are applied to the dealings with a person in the present. In counselling, it is the process whereby the client brings their unconscious unprocessed feelings and experiences and re-enacts them in the counselling sessions. Klein (1952) in her work with children considered that transference occurs in a therapeutic relationship because the client has formed an attachment to her counsellor. It is not surprising that Jane, as the person closest to Denise, is the person who bears the brunt of Denise's unconscious communications of pushing her away and showing angry behaviour.

A client who was referred to me, Mr Evans, came to his first assessment session on his own. He took great care to tell me how he had worked out his route, and had managed not to get lost. However, when he reached the clinic he became overwhelmed by its size. He talked about how long the corridors were and how confusing the building was. He told me anxiously that he had seen a small child wandering around in the corridor, apparently looking for his parents. He was concerned about this child; will he find his parents? Have they even noticed he is missing? I think Mr Evans was communicating through the transference his feelings of being a lost child, his anxieties that he would not be able to make the journey to reach me without getting lost, and his worry that I would not even notice if he did not turn up for his appointment.

Klein's contributions to psychodynamic counselling

Melanie Klein pioneered the psychoanalytic understanding and treatment of children. Her work built on the knowledge gained by Freud in his work with adults, and she is responsible for many important developments in our understanding of *personality development*. She particularly concentrated on the development of the relationship between an infant and the significant people around him or her, particularly mother, from birth onwards. Klein identified processes in early infancy that impact on an individual's personality development, how they subsequently see them-selves and their relationships with others. She identified, through watching children at play, the idea that children develop internal representations of relationships with significant others, coloured by their own impulses, that affect their everyday interactions. She called these internal representations '*object relations*'. She saw these internalisations not as actual copies, but as having the ability to take on their own internal life and to create their own internal relationships.

Although this is primarily a book about working with adults, its premise is that events and relationships from birth, and par-ticularly those in early childhood, are critical in understanding the many facets of personality, particularly the aspects which impinge on how adversity is managed. Klein's work sheds much light on some of the processes that can occur between an infant born with an obvious disability and his primary carers, even though she did not write directly about disability. Through exploring 'normal development' Klein was able to illustrate some of the long-term emotional consequences for an individual where there have been early difficulties in the relationship between infant and main carer.

Object relations theory

Melanie Klein's theory of object relations was developed through careful observation of many children at play, and children's inter-actions with others. Her detailed observations enabled her to hypothesise about internal processes, such as children's wishes, dreams, fantasies, hopes, fears and expectations. Like Freud, she emphasised the importance of unconscious *phantasies* (the spelling indicates an unconscious process as opposed to fantasy which is considered conscious) and Klein believed these were occurring from birth in a primitive form. Based on her theories, she developed a play technique for children (Klein, 1923) which has been the foundation for the practice of child psychotherapy. She viewed the way children play as an unconscious communi-cation and as having symbolic meaning, much the same way as Freud understood his patient's free associations and dreams. She understood how the early infantile feelings of the children she worked with were transferred onto their relationship with her, and this understanding allowed her to recognise what some of these early infantile processes must have been. From this understanding she developed and refined a theory of normal emotional development from birth.

The paranoid–schizoid position

According to Klein, an infant is subject to extreme fluctuations in mental state or emotions from birth. His experience will be a series of sensations both internal and external such as hunger, tiredness, being cuddled, being fed or bathed. When he is hungry, tired, thirsty, hot, cold, in pain, he is unable to understand what is causing the discomfort, or to predict when, if ever, the discomfort will go. In the same way, the infant will be unable to predict when positive experiences will occur, and this lack of understanding can cause extreme *persecutory anxieties*. He will try to modify his experience in the only ways he can, so when he experiences extreme anxieties he will try to evacuate or expel these bad feelings just as he does faeces or urine. At these times, his world is experienced as devastatingly bad, he experiences the discomfort as persecutory or as a *nameless dread* (Bion, 1962a). His carer, or mother (Klein focused her work mostly on the relationship with the infant's mother), responds to his distress, and in most cases she can alleviate it. When the hungry baby is fed, his world is transformed and any bad, attacking, angry feelings he experienced miraculously dissipate. All is well again, until the next experience of discomfort. Klein noticed that for the first four to seven months of an infant's life, he is unable to tolerate discomfort, and his mother seems to be experienced as either all bad, withholding and persecutory, or all good, giving and protecting. It is as if the infant experiences the mother as separate people or *part objects*, either wholly good or wholly bad. The infant's world is fragmented, and in phantasy he will try to protect himself and his objects by either exaggerating the good and denying the possibility of bad aspects to his good objects, and similarly deny the good, and exaggerate the possibility of negative aspects to his bad objects. This process of *idealisation* can result in rapid changes in the perception of objects, when for example, a good object does not provide what is expected of it, it can suddenly be transformed into a bad, withholding or persecuting object.

Klein described how the defensive process of idealisation consists of the defences of *splitting* and *denial*. She also recognised that these defences can occur at any point in a persons' life, they are not just confined to infancy. She saw this pattern of experience, where the mother is split, in the infant's mind, into all good or all bad as depending on the infants' immediate experience, as the first distinct developmental stage or position, to which she gave the name *'the paranoid schizoid position'*. One of the most important concepts from this understanding of intrapsychic processes is that of *projective identification*. This is when in phantasy good or bad aspects of a person are split off and projected into an external object, and then this object or part object is identified with those aspects of the self. Klein saw this process as a way of the infant trying to join up with the object, as a way of denying any separation; through the process of projective identification the infant becomes merged with external objects. This defence or way of communicating can continue to be utilised throughout life.

The depressive position

When all goes well, as the infant grows and develops he becomes more able to anticipate that his needs can or will be met. This leads to an ability to start to tolerate distress and frustration. This development does not occur in isolation; the infant can only start to anticipate his needs being met if his experience is that, more or less, his needs are met. Winnicott (1962) referred to this relationship as *holding*, which he saw as encompassing both the physical care and emotional environment that a mother provides for her children. Both Klein and Winnicott stressed the importance of allowing the infant the opportunity to develop the resources to manage the gap between a need, and having that need met. Importantly, as he develops and learns, he becomes increasingly able to fill the gap of frustration himself, with the internal imagined idea of, for example, a breast and being fed. This development is the *origin of a thought*, and this process is the origin of thinking. The absence of what the infant wants or needs forces a thought to occur and the process of thinking to begin.

As the infant grows he starts to realise that his idealised mother does not always meet his needs, and in fact the good mother, and the bad, withholding mother are actually one and the same. This realisation leads the infant to experience feelings of guilt and *depressive anxieties* over his more negative impulses. Depressive anxieties are mobilised by separations, loss and in infancy the process of weaning. When his mother is absent, he can feel that he has damaged her with his negative, aggressive feelings. He starts to experience reparation wishes as he understands that his angry, often attacking feelings have been directed at the mother whom he loves, not just the bad mother; as they are one and the same person. Not only does he experience feelings of guilt, but he is able to feel remorse and suffering for his mother. When his mother returns undamaged, the infant is able to develop a more realistic idea about his emotions, and the impact they can have on other people or objects, and his ability to repair damage. Over time and with continuing losses that he must manage, he develops a stronger sense of himself. Klein called this stage or process, where the infant is able to recognise whole people or objects as separate, the *depressive position*. The depressive position is characterised by guilt and anxiety, as ambivalent feelings are recognised as such, and reparative, loving and altruistic feelings are mobilised. This state of mind characterises mature relationships and is associated with the internal processes of *reparation* and *introjection* (taking in the good aspects of another). It is a lifelong task to strive for the management of depressive anxieties, as events, losses and change can generate infantile feelings or responses.

Although the paranoid-schizoid and depressive processes have been described as stages, Klein saw them as positions (hence their titles) that could be moved in and out of throughout child and adulthood, as a result of change and adversity (both internal and external). Different kinds of conflicts or anxieties arise in these different positions, and Klein identified a number of *defences* that we employ to protect our core selves or objects, against such difficulties.

Defences

Identifying and thinking about defence mechanisms is an important aspect of counselling, and can help clients recognise unhelpful unconscious processes at play that may be hindering their development. In the counselling relationship, defences can be identified both through the transference relationship and through aspects of what a person says and does. Bateman and Holmes (1995) summarise the range of defences that counsellors are interested in identifying and exploring with their clients. They describe how some defences, such as idealisation, projection and projective identification are more primitive, originating in an earlier developmental stage than others. Defences such as denial, dissociation, regression and repression are seen to be more *neurotic* defences. Another way of grouping defensive processes is to associate the range of *omnipotent* defences (states of mind where the child fears that its thoughts and phantasies can alter the external world) together as *manic defences*. This grouping would include denial, control and idealisation. There are also defences that are more commonly employed by people with learning disabilities such as secondary and opportunist handicaps and we will look at the use of these defences in more detail later. The use of defences is not necessarily problematic or pathological, as we all employ them to cope with any distresses that our internal and external worlds throw at us. Defences protect us against uncomfortable and painful feelings and are therefore a necessary and important aspect of our functioning. Problems only arise when defences are over-rigidly used, or employed in such a way that they prevent our development or interfere with aspects of our functioning. So, for example, if an infant cuts off from interactions with a carer because the interactions are particularly painful, this will hinder his or her ability to make other relationships.

Meltzer (1968), and Alvarez (1992) have written about the effects of using certain defences too rigidly, from an early age when the development of self is immature and vulnerable. It is possible that these defences can become integrated into a person's personality structure and fixed as such. In these cases it can be more difficult, but not impossible, for change and development to take place. In the case of people with learning disabilities, there is a possibility that defensive processes can contribute towards the difficulties in learning; that is, thinking can be impeded by emotional difficulties. It is through the work of Wilfred Bion that we have developed our understanding of these complex processes.

Bion and the development of thinking

Wilfred Bion developed Klein's ideas regarding infant development and made important connections between infantile early experience and intellectual development. Bion was interested in the functioning of groups and organisations. He was also very interested in Klein's ideas about the development of thinking. Klein had put forward the idea that the gap between having a need, such as hunger pains, and having the need met can cause a frustration that can lead to the infant creating the idea of a feed, a breast, that can hold him together, to keep himself from experiencing disintegration, until the feed arrives.

Esther Bick explored in detail how a mother is able to hold her infant not only physically, but also in her mind. By thinking about him, she pulls together all the aspects of himself, and by doing so helps him learn to focus his attention (Bick, 1968). Bick noticed how an infant will focus intensely on an aspect of his environment, such as a light or a noise, as a way of keeping himself together. She hypothesised that this was to stop him from feeling that he is falling apart or disintegrating. As he grows, and he has enough experience of being held, both physically and emotionally, he will internalise the ability to hold himself together. As Bick described, he will start to develop a sense that his skin is literally holding him together in a way which she calls a *psychic skin*. With this development, he becomes a being who is together enough to take in or introject aspects of others. He also develops a sense that his mother has enough of a containing psychic skin to be able to tolerate his projections.

Bion focused on this ability of a mother to tolerate her infant's projections in his work on containment. He introduced the concept of the mother being a *container* for the infants' distressing or uncomfortable feelings. So, for example, the infant is distressed because he is hungry. He finds the distress unbearable and he throws it out or *projects* it into anyone who is available. Infants are especially good at projecting their distress, and this is why it is so hard to ignore the cries of a baby in distress. When things go well, his mother is able to comfort and feed her baby because she has a sense of the distress he is feeling. She is able to identify with the infant's feelings, to introject them and she is able to *think about* the experience of her infant, responding to meet his needs. Because she is able to allow herself to be in touch with his feelings, she shows him that his feelings are tolerable. In other words she transforms his distressed feelings by taking them in, and by responding to him she transforms and returns them to him in a modified form. It is as if by thinking for her child, the mother shows him that thinking is possible, and how it is done. Bion described this process as *containment*; he saw the mother or any carer as a *container*, and the infant as being *contained*. He described this process as being vital in an infants' early life, but as continuing in various forms throughout life. For example, a good friend who listens to your problems can lighten your load just by containing your feelings, just as a good (or effective) counsellor acts as a container to his or her client's projected feelings, and is able to modify them by thinking about them. However, counsellors differ from friends in that they may also make interpretations or comments to elucidate unconscious processes. Through the process of containment the client is then able to take back or introject the modified and processed feelings.

The relevance of these ideas to working with people with learning disabilities is immense. There is a large literature relating to the experience of parents when their child is born disabled; some writers view it as a bereavement, a loss of the 'normal' child, others as a trauma (Bicknell, 1983). What is clear is that however loving parents are, the birth of a child with a disability is a shock that needs to be processed. When parents have to manage their own feelings, it is hard to be fully available to their infant's experience. While parents are trying to make sense of their child's difficulties and their responses to these, they may at times find it more difficult to be able to think about or to contain their infants' emotions or projections. This is not to say that parents of children with disabilities are likely to be neglectful, or that all children born with disabilities cause their parents such distress that they become temporarily emotionally unavailable. It is, however, a possibility that difficulties may occur.

Donald Winnicott wrote of how a mother's face mirrors her feelings for her infant. Her face and eyes reflect her love and concern, he can see in her gaze, her voice and her touch, himself as a perfect, loved person (Winnicott, 1965). When a child is born with a disability the reflection may be tainted with the mother's fluctuating response to her child. As one mother of a daughter born with Down's Syndrome told me: 'I'm not sure that I can hide from her how upset I feel at times, my fears for the future, even though I do really love her'.

As Sinason (1992) said 'when a child (handicapped or not) is not wanted, it sees a different message in its parents' eyes. There is no gleaming light or twinkle that says you are loveable; there is coldness, hurt, shame, hate, fear, anger'. Sinason points out that for many disabled children, loving relationships with their parents or carers are achieved. However, when the relationship is rejecting, it can be taken in as an unwanted negative sense of self or object that can impact on all future relationships.

Psychodynamic counselling and learning disabilities

The misconception that verbal skills are necessary in order for a person to benefit from psychodynamic treatments has been quite pervasive. As recently as 1979, Brown and Pedder indicated that a certain degree of intelligence was required to use counselling forms of treatment. Beail (1995b) has reviewed the literature over recent years and discovered that the exclusion criteria has existed to varying degrees over time, and that this exclusion seems more complicated than just an omission or a failure to translate the approach for the learning disabled. Ferenczi (1929) describes how people with learning disabilities are thought about in therapeutic work as 'unwelcome guests of the family'. He goes on to explore why this might be the case. He describes how people with learning disabilities can come to represent a receptacle for feelings of hatred or disability in their families. The learning disabled person then becomes *projected* into, and Ferenczi thought that this led to their susceptibility to minor physical ailments such as coughs and colds, and more significant illnesses such as epilepsy. It is likely that this process is not just confined within families, but that wider society projects feelings of inadequacy, disability, ugliness and insecurity into the section of the population who represent disability. If we were to acknowledge the psychological pain that people with disabilities can and do feel, we would have to recognise our own weaknesses. It is safer to see people with disabilities as different and separate from the norm. The use of people with disabilities as 'buckets for projection', is probably the main reason why this group has been excluded from 'talking' treatments. Other popular reasons for this marked exclusion include the belief that they do not have the language or cognitive ability to understand talking treatments, or that cognitive impairment equates with emotional impairment; that is, feelings are impaired alongside the disability.

Even though they are an unpopular population, there are a number of theorists and clinicians who have persevered in trying to understand the inner world of people with disabilities, and more recently our understanding has been greatly increased by authors such as Bicknell, Frankish, Hollins and Sinason.

The work of Sinason and colleagues

Valerie Sinason trained as a child psychotherapist, but she was quick to see how psychodynamic theories and treatments could be helpful to both adults and children with learning disabilities. With a colleague at the Tavistock Clinic in London, Jon Stokes (1987) she described how cognitive and emotional intelligence are not necessarily linked, and that it is possible for emotional intelligence to develop age appropriately whilst still having severe cognitive impairment. The reverse is also true; it is possible to be very intelligent, but to struggle with emotions, both in recognising and experiencing feelings. They used the term 'emotional intelligence' as a helpful way of differentiating the thinking and the feeling aspects of a person. This is not to say that the two develop completely independently, or that changes in one area do not have an impact on the other, but rather to recognise that they can exist independently of each other.

CASE EXAMPLE: Angela

An adolescent that I worked with, Angela, had a condition that resulted in a severe learning disability, and a marked physical disability. Her eyes were lopsided, and her nose had not properly formed, making her facial features quite noticeably different. She was also unable to walk very far, so was normally wheelchair-bound. The staff at her school commented that although she appeared to be unresponsive and unaware about what happened around her, the other day they had been out on a school trip and noticed that when they took photos she turned away. At first it was considered to be a coincidence that she turned at this point, as she often has facial spasms, but the staff soon realised that this was consistent behaviour, whenever a photo was taken of her, she turned away. The staff were surprised, they did not think either that she had that degree of control over her movement, or that photographs had any meaning for her. She may or may not have understood what a photo was, but she clearly did have an emotional understanding of how painful it is to look different, how hurtful it is to be different. Capturing this difference on film was painful for Angela. Her cognitive development may have been at around the six-month old level, but she had the feelings of an adolescent girl, who wanted to be attractive, and who was aware of how other people might view her.

Another Tavistock Clinic worker, Neville Symington, published a very early case study of psychotherapy with a learning disabled man (Symington, 1981). His work with Harry, a man in his early thirties who was struggling with violent tantrums, raised some very important questions about intelligence such as 'what is intelligence?' 'What factors can modify the use of intelligence?' His work with Harry raised an important dilemma in working with people with disabilities; Harry became more able to express his feelings, but with this, he became more unco-operative with staff working with him. Symington made a comparison with a published case study of a man who became depressed when he recovered his sight. This is a common concern in this work. As people shed their secondary handicaps and become more able to express their feelings, they are likely to become more in touch with their reality and often this leads to depression. Sinason (1997) describes how important it is to allow an adequate amount of time for this kind of work, as the core difficulties may only be reached after a year or so, and stopping treatment prematurely may leave the client with their depression exposed, and reduced means to defend against its devastating effects.

At the same time as the developments in working psychodynamically with people with learning disabilities at the Tavistock Clinic were occurring there were other clinicians also developing strands of specialist interest elsewhere. At St George's Hospital in London, Joan Bicknell published an important paper focusing on the impact of feelings of loss for the learning disabled person and their parents (Bicknell, 1983). She explored how these feelings can impact on early development and relationships between people with learning disabilities and their families, and that this impact can have ongoing consequences. A colleague of hers, Sheila Hollins developed ideas with Sinason about people with disabilities' fear of unconscious death wishes, the fear that people around them would prefer that they hadn't been born, or that they would just die or go away (Sinason and Hollins, 2000). She also has undertaken considerable research on the impact of bereavement and loss on people with learning disabilities, and concludes that these are very significant issues for this client group, and that often their importance is minimised or ignored.

In the Midlands two psychologists, Pat Frankish and Nigel Beail, contributed to the developing field. Frankish demonstrated how Mahler's ideas about psychological birth and development could be applied to counselling with people with learning disabilities (Frankish, 1992), and Beail worked on demonstrating the effectiveness of counselling with this client group (see Chapter 9).

From all this important work, it is apparent that there has been a gradual climate change towards providing talking treatments for people with disabilities, and that they are no longer judged as a uniform group who are unable to benefit. With this increased interest has come the development of our understanding of some of the psychological processes that appear to be associated with disability.

Although Freud's work was not written with people with learning disabilities specifically in mind, he did develop some theoretical ideas which have been very helpful for work in this field. Freud's (1901) concept of 'secondary gain', contributed towards the recognition of the process of secondary handicap (Sinason, 1992). Freud described the idea of secondary gain as being the process whereby a person's symptoms are used to their advantage. This idea had resonance with Sinason and Stokes's work on the defensive process of *secondary handicap* often utilised by people with learning disabilities. Secondary handicap is a process that occurs when original or primary disability is exaggerated as a way of defending one's self against the painful feelings of difference, thereby making other people 'stupid' for not realising this is an exaggeration. So in secondary handicap, people might consciously or unconsciously exaggerate aspects of their disabilities, such as voice, movements or body distortion, in order to have control over the disability and over other people; they have a 'secret triumph' over their fooling everyone else, they are not really that handicapped (Sinason, 1997). It takes a degree of openness to emotional responses to be able to understand and see beyond these processes in working with people with learning disabilities.

CASE EXAMPLE: Jamila

A young woman, Jamila, was referred for counselling by her keyworker at her day centre because she had been behaving more aggressively. Jamila has moderate learning disabilities, and she has been attending the centre for the last six years where the staff report that she has been 'no trouble'. She was brought to the clinic by a worker from the centre who said 'she is a little deaf so you will need to talk loudly and if you use Makaton (sign language) it will help'. Jamila sat in the room avoiding eye contact with the counsellor, who talked (loudly and self consciously) about how Jamila might be feeling about coming to the clinic. Jamila did not respond but started whining loudly to herself. The counsellor had a strong sense that Jamila didn't trust her, and she said, in her normal voice that she thought Jamila was finding it difficult being with her, and that Jamila might not quite believe that the counsellor would want to know her or to be with her. Jamila looked at the counsellor with some curiosity and said clearly and with obvious intelligence 'you're right, people don't really want to listen to me'. Jamila may have some hearing loss but she demonstrated how she could hear normal tone with no difficulty. Jamila seemed to be exaggerating her difficulties to manage feelings she was having about being learning disabled, and this use of a secondary handicap was certainly adding to her disabilities.

Sinason's ideas about the processes, such as secondary handicap, occuring in people with disabilities have been extremely important. She started to provide psychotherapy to people with learning disabilities when the climate was still very behaviourally and medically inclined. Through her extensive clinical work, she has developed an understanding of some of the common issues and themes that arise in this work, and has identified five key areas of conflict or difficulty that appear to be associated with a learning disability. These themes are:

• the disability itself;
• loss;
• dependency needs;
• sexuality;
• the fear of being murdered.
(Sinason, 1999, Sinason and Hollins, 2000)

These themes are indeed pervasive and arise in much of the work with people with learning disabilities. It is worth bearing them in mind whilst looking at the case examples throughout this text, as at least one theme described above can be identified in all the examples given.

SUMMARY

• This chapter has drawn attention to the central importance of psychoanalytic theory in understanding the inner worlds of people with learning disabilities. This has been a brief account and the reader will find a fuller account in several good texts, for example Hinshelwood (1991), Bateman and Holmes (1995), Rycroft (1972).

- A key understanding relevant to counselling adults with learning disabilities is that everyone has an unconscious world, built up of object relations that impact on our daily lives. However, when conflict occurs within these worlds, defences are mobilised, and occasionally these defences, and the conflict itself, can create emotional, behavioural and cognitive difficulties.

- Another important understanding is that unconscious processes can be identified through the processes of transference and countertransference, tools that help us understand people's inner worlds.

- In order to be able to reflect on unconscious processes, we must be able to think about our own inner worlds, and the best way of doing this is through personal psychotherapy or analysis. Proper supervision is also very important in the process of teasing out what each person brings to a counselling relationship.

3

Assessment and the Beginnings of a Therapeutic Relationship

In this chapter we will look at assessment for counselling, and how to utilise psychodynamic ideas in other kinds of assessments. Assessment is a process of information gathering and trying to make sense of something; the *Oxford English Dictionary* (9th edn, 1997) defines it as 'to estimate or evaluate the quality of'. Assessment can be an ongoing process, and does not have to be defined as taking place only within the first meetings. If, in our clinical work, we make ongoing efforts to think about our responses to our clients, and their responses to us, we are constantly evaluating or making assessments. This process is different to the more formal assessment for counselling described below.

Firstly we will consider the benefits of maintaining a questioning and evaluative stance in all clinical work, from direct hands-on work through to more irregular contact. It is helpful to have a flexible attitude towards assessment, and to always take a thoughtful, reflective stance towards all interactions with people with learning disabilities. If assessment is seen in terms of a specific task within a specific time frame, for example, to try to find out 'why' a person self-injures, using only a few brief meetings or contacts, then important understandings might be missed. Fluctuating states and moods may be 'boxed' in to a rigid understanding or diagnosis.

If we continue to question in our minds what a client makes us feel and to think about our responses to the people we work with, we are more likely to gain deeper understandings of their internal worlds. For example, Emma is a residential social worker in a group home for four people with severe learning disabilities. When she started to work in the home, she was given 'factual' information about each resident, so she was told 'this is Tom, he has a tendency to lash out for no reason, this is Sarah, she loves watching soaps. This is Frank he's a bit of a joker, he loves to wind us all up, and Gillian here, takes no notice of us'. These statements assume that the people who live in the home are all predictable and consistent. Whilst it is important to communicate important information, the likes and dislikes of individuals, accepting every aspect of the collective wisdom may not necessarily help one's own understanding of a particular client. For example, Emma was at work watching all the residents at a meal time. She was spoon feeding Gillian as she understood that Gillian could not feed herself. This was frustrating as Gillian had the knack of jerking her head just as the spoon entered her mouth, frequently sending its contents down her front. Emma was curious about this. It was so regular and consistent that she started to wonder if it wasn't just a coincidence. These thoughts were occurring to her as she held the spoon in front of Gillian's mouth, and she became quite absorbed, forgetting her current task. She was brought back to the present with a jolt when Gillian placed her hand over Emma's and directed the spoon into her mouth. Emma was fascinated. She thought Gillian was always totally passive in the process of being fed. Through thinking about this interaction, and evaluating Gillian's behaviour, Emma felt she had gained a different understanding of Gillian and over time this allowed her to add more variety to Gillian's day, starting with the kinds of foods she ate and how her food was presented. The small communication Gillian made was facilitated by Emma's sensitive and thoughtful observations.

Assessment in different settings

Therapeutic contact does not have to be confined to a set counselling appointment, many workers do not have the luxury of arranging contained therapy sessions. For example, front-line staff such as nurses and residential workers, even with the best will, may not be able to offer a protected space for individual counselling. However, useful work can take place just by taking the time to think about clients behaviour, what it might be communicating or what inner states might be associated with certain behaviours, such as Emma demonstrated in the above example. Considering one's countertransference responses will also give important indications as to the nature of a person's object relations and defences.

Formal assessment for counselling: referrals and the aim of assessment

It is unusual for a people with learning disabilities to refer themselves for counselling. It is much more likely that a carer, or another professional, instigates the referral. The most common reasons for referral are to do with behaviour, with concerns about aggressive or odd behaviour topping the list, normally because the behaviour is a problem for someone else. It is more unusual for anxiety or depression to be the sole reason for a referral. This is probably because it is easier to overlook *negative symptoms* such as being withdrawn and uncommunicative in a population who are more likely to have difficulty in expressing themselves. There is also a much higher rate of referral for the consequences of abuse, especially sexual abuse, which is unsurprising given the higher incidence of abuse towards people with learning disabilities (Craft, 1994).

What then is the aim of an assessment for counselling? How might the counsellor's aims be different to the aims of the referrer and other professionals working with the client? Given referrals frequently make references to difficult behaviour, it would seem that a common aim of the referrer is to reduce such behaviour. However, this may not be an aim of the referred patient, or an explicit aim of the counsellor, and can lead to misunderstandings or unhelpful interactions.

A central aim of the counsellor is to reduce the negative impacts or unhelpful defences against internal conflict, by helping the client to recognise and think about unconscious dynamics that are at play. This aim is hopefully achieved by making internal objects, inner worlds and their workings, more available or accessible to the client. It is hoped that by doing so, any distress a person is experiencing will be reduced. It is not necessarily the explicit aim that the client's behaviour will be changed, although it is hoped that identifying the meaning in behaviours will allow for a more helpful expression of feelings. This was apparent, as discussed in Chapter 2, with Symington's patient, Harry, who became more able to express his feelings and, as a result became more assertive and difficult with the staff in his ATC (Symington, 1981). As part of the assessment it is important to clarify with the referrer and significant others about any expectations for treatment, so that such misunderstandings are not created.

CASE EXAMPLE: Ms Brown

Ms Brown is a thirty-eight-year-old woman with moderate learning disabilities. She lives in a residential home for eight people. Staff in the home noticed that at the beginning and end of the week, particularly Mondays and Fridays, Ms Brown is more agitated and restless than at other times. Every other weekend she returns to her parent's home for the weekend. The manager of the home referred Ms Brown for counselling for her agitated behaviour. He checked with Ms Brown's parents about making the referral, and they were supportive, as they too felt that she was becoming unusually withdrawn on her visits. The counsellor met with Ms Brown who was very reluctant to talk, saying she didn't want to meet with the counsellor unless her parents came. The counsellor felt in a dilemma, should she invite the parents to a meeting? Would it feel like she was treating Ms Brown like a child? She decided that as Ms Brown had expressed a clear wish for her parents to attend, that she would organise a meeting for them all together. In this meeting Mr and Mrs Brown were initially very focused on the question of 'what is wrong with our daughter?' but as they talked further it became clear that they had a number of difficulties of their own. Ms Brown watched her parents with interest as they talked about the financial difficulties they were experiencing since Mr Brown's redundancy and the strain this had put on their relationship. Mrs Brown started to cry as she talked about how she had moved into the spare room (Ms Brown's old room) and how she and her husband never seemed to find the time to talk about their difficulties. The counsellor suggested that they be referred for couple counselling, which they both agreed to with apparent relief. Ms Brown was much calmer after this meeting. It seemed as if her 'symptoms' were an expression of her parents' difficulties. Accepting her behaviour as problematic and treating her individually would have been unlikely to have had any significant impact on her behaviour.

Counselling is a two-person, two-way relationship. Therefore the client is not just a recipient, but an active participant in the process. As Jung (1946) put it, psychotherapy is a 'conjunction' or a symbolic mingling of minds. An aim of assessment is firstly to explore if this is understood by the client, and secondly if it is indeed possible. Orlinsky and Howard (1986) described three key features of a therapeutic relationship that are positively correlated with a good outcome. These are:

- the ability to form a good rapport or working relationship
- the ability to work with interpretations
- the capacity to respond affectively with in sessions; to be able to access and express feelings of anger, fear or sadness

We are therefore looking for indications that the client can use a psychodynamic approach; that they want to attempt to make a link, to take a chance on thinking about their distress. We are also trying to make some preliminary formulations about the origin and maintaining factors of the client's difficulties. This requires collecting information from the client about historical factors, life events and stages that are contributing to their difficulties. There are two main strands to consider in assessment, which Bateman and Holmes (1995) refer to as objective (history) and subjective (the creation of a constructive therapeutic relationship). I think that there are four central aspects to accessing these two areas, and to making a thorough assessment for therapy. These are:

- taking as detailed and accurate history as is possible,
- detailed observation,
- setting up a therapeutic environment taking communication considerations into account,
- evaluating a client's response to a psychodynamic approach.

We shall look at each of these four areas in turn.

History taking

People with learning disabilities, their families and carers are all too familiar with the idea of assessments. From the early days, when a difficulty with learning was first detected, or even from pregnancy and birth when a disability may have been identified, every professional that the person meets will want to make some kind of assessment. From the health visitor, doctor, physiotherapist, speech therapist, teacher, psychologist, psychiatrist to social worker, everyone will have a different perspective, different questions that need answers or data that needs to be collected. With good practice, each assessment will be recorded so that the client, their family and professionals have access to the thoughts of the assessor. However, this can create reams of information. One mother of a thirty-two year old daughter who had been referred for an assessment for counselling brought two over-flowing box files of reports to our first meeting, saying that she hoped it might save me some time! This is not an unusual occurrence, and of course it is important to have a thorough understanding of each client's health, medical and social history. However, paper 'stories' can be inaccurate, misleading and biased. They are written from the author's particular perspective, which may be very different from a psychodynamic viewpoint. Excessive documentation can also be used in a defensive way, to create a distance from more distressing or painful aspects of functioning.

CASE EXAMPLE: Louise

Louise is an eighteen-year-old woman with moderate learning disabilities who was referred for counselling because of recently developing uncharacteristic mood swings and difficult behaviour at her special school. A plan had been developed that, on finishing school, she should attend the local further education college one day a week to build on her daily living skills. Louise's social worker had made the referral to our team with Louise's parents' consent, because she was concerned that Louise was jeopardising her placement at the college with her difficult behaviour. Enclosed with the referral letter was a paediatric review report dated about five years previously that gave a brief history. It stated that: 'Louise was born at forty-two weeks. Normal delivery. No post natal problems. Breastfed. Concerns raised at eight month check that Louise was hypotonic (*floppy*), lacked alertness and no babbling. Referral to child development services for full assessment at eighteen months as health visitor still concerned about general developmental delay. Diagnosis of moderate learning disability made at three years.'

Louise attended her first assessment appointment accompanied by her mother, Mrs Clark. Louise asked for her mother to stay with her for this meeting. Louise sat close to her mother, looking to her before speaking, as if she needed approval. During this interview we talked about Louise's early life, her mother's pregnancy, Louise's birth and her early days. Mrs Clark said that her pregnancy with Louise had been very difficult, she had been extremely sick and she had a number of anxious weeks owing to unexplained bleeds. Louise's birth had been very difficult, she was induced because Louise was overdue, the labour was long and painful, and the birth was eventually assisted with forceps. She described how she wanted to breastfeed Louise, but she had been fretful and wasn't able to latch on properly. Mrs Clark talked in a flat unemotional tone about how she had given up trying to breastfeed when Louise was two weeks, and moved her on to bottled milk. Louise shrunk closer to her mother as Mrs Clark continued talking in the same flat, detached way about how difficult she had found Louise as a baby, always crying and hard to settle. She described how she and her husband had originally planned to have more than one child, but she did not feel able to have any more following the difficulties with Louise, saying 'I couldn't bear to go through it again'.

At this meeting it was clear just how much important information would have been missed if the medical report had been accepted at face value. Louise's birth story was recorded as fact, but her experience as told by her mother in the meeting was very different to the record, demonstrating the importance of making one's own assessment.

It is important to get as accurate history as is possible. Early events can be incorporated or introjected in such a way that they can continue to have an impact on functioning throughout life. Whenever possible it is most helpful to get personal history from the client themselves. This will give an opportunity to gain an indication of how previous events have been experienced, or indeed are currently thought about. However, many clients are unable to communicate or remember their past experiences accurately for physical cognitive, or emotional reasons. They may not have been told clearly about events because people close to them have felt that 'it is for the best'. For example, a thirty-year old woman's mother told me that her daughter had undergone a hysterectomy when she was thirteen years old and that she had not been told the reason for her operation. Similarly a man in his fifties seen by our team was not told about the fact his father had terminal cancer, because his mother felt it would cause him too much distress. Interestingly, in both these cases, as is invariably the way, both these people knew, at some level, what they were not supposed to know. The woman told me, 'you know I can't have babies don't you?' and the man spent the therapy sessions after his father's diagnosis talking about how devastated he felt when his sister left home. Something had triggered in him a memory, thought or experience of how it feels when significant others are no longer around.

When it is not possible to get a direct history from the client, other ways of collecting information need to be found. Reports from involved professionals can be one such way. It can be helpful to meet with the professional system to hear from them their perspectives and understandings of the client. Talking to the referrer (and to the GP if they are different people) is important for several reasons, such as collecting relevant information as getting a sense of the context of the referral. The 'why now?' and 'why counselling?' questions can be helpful to tease out the relationship between the referrer and the client.

Sometimes it can be helpful to meet the client together with the referrer, to explore the understandings between them regarding the referral. On other occasions it can be helpful to have a case conference prior to seeing the client for the first time. A case conference or network meeting, where all the significant professionals working with a client meet together, is often useful when the referrer is unclear about why this particular client could use counselling, or when there are real doubts about whether the client can use a talking approach. Kahr (1997) highlights the importance of enlisting the co-operation of the referrer and the client's family because they ultimately have the final say about whether the patient attends therapy or not.

Clients' families can also be helpful sources of information, although talking to families raises dilemmas regarding confidentiality, the danger of perpetuating a client's infantilisation, or undermining their independence. One way to minimise these possibilities is to work in pairs, to co-work. When a client has given permission, or it is seen as necessary for either the client or the relatives, one worker can see the client, whilst the other worker sees the relatives.

Although some clients may come with detailed assessment histories either because of extensive contact with professionals or because they have families who can speak for them, it may not always be the case. It is not uncommon for people with learning disabilities to have no, or minimal, available documented history, especially older adults or people with a history of institutional care (McCormack, 1991). McCormack argues that the absence of a person's history is tantamount to a denial of a person's identity and therefore the meaning in their lives. He points out that on a wide scale this has the impact of more generally denying the significance of events in people with learning disabilities lives, thus perpetuating the poor recording of their histories.

There is a fine line to tread when trying to decide how much information to obtain prior to, or at the beginning of, an assessment. It is possible to be overwhelmed by paper reports, or to know absolutely nothing about the client's background prior to the first meeting with them. Both these situations can muddy the waters in making a helpful assessment for counselling. Too much information can be unhelpful; it can be irrelevant or misleading. Too little information means important events in a person's history may be ignored or their impact and meaning minimised.

Observation

In any assessment, observation is a critical tool. However, in an assessment for therapy, the observation is not solely of behaviours, but of the states of mind that accompany them, and of the states of mind and feelings that are evoked in others by any observable behaviours. This was brought home to me in a very powerful way when I was completing my own training. I was asked to see a young woman, Carley, who had severe learning disabilities and who regularly self-injured in a horrific way. Carley's arms were in splints because she poked at her face and eyes to the extent that she had completely lost the use of her left eye. Her face and scalp were often red, raw and weeping from the injuries she inflicted. She was described as having no sense of pain, and the staff in her residential hospital felt that they had 'tried everything' to stop her injuring herself. They described how they had tried many behavioural techniques such as reward and positive reinforcement, but nothing had reduced the frequency of the self-attacks.

I felt very anxious about seeing Carley individually and about being able to help her. At the time, I found it difficult to reflect on what this anxiety may have been related to, such as Carley's own feelings being so unthought about and uncontained. I asked the staff to think about, and monitor what happened when Carley self-injured, what she was doing, when she did it, what was going on around her, and how the staff experienced Carley at these times. Interestingly when I returned to the hospital a week later to find out what had developed, the ward sister took me aside and said that they had tried to make some kind of a recording about Carley's self-injury, but there was 'nothing to report'. She showed me a chart with the times of her self-injury and little boxes next to them all saying 'no reason, nothing any different happening'. It was almost as if Carley's behaviour was just too painful to think about.

To start with, I felt incredibly helpless, perhaps there was nothing that I could do or suggest that would make any difference to Carley. I then became aware of being made to feel defeated and stupid. This created in me feelings of anger and defiance. All of these feelings occurred in quick succession, but were very powerful. Being able to reflect on them helped me enormously, not just with my assessment of Carley, but in understanding the nature of observation. In making an observation of a client for therapy, the observation is not just of events, behaviours, times, but of one's own response, and the response that is evoked in the client by this response and so on. It is impossible to describe an observation without using emotive language, without including oneself in the observation.

Carley's ward sister agreed for me to join a handover meeting, where the residents were being discussed. When we all talked together about the process of observing Carley, we were able to reflect on the feelings she evoked in all of us, and I was interested to hear that other people described some of the feelings that I had experienced when being with Carley. Staff seemed to fluctuate between frustrated helplessness and anger when thinking about her. This discussion generated some ideas about what might be going on for Carley, and some indications about what her self-injury might be related to. One thoughtful nursing assistant, Claire, said, 'I didn't put it on the chart, because it wasn't something that happened to Carley. On Wednesday when Eve's sister was visiting her, Carley had her splints off and she started to jab at her eyes. I hate it when she does that – it makes me feel so helpless. She jabbed away, without seeming to feel anything. I can't bear to look when she does that'. Another staff member picked up on her use of language 'you can't bear to look and she's the one blinding herself', and yet a third staff made a link to the visitor, saying that Carley had never had a visitor, it was as if no one cared about her, or remembered her existence. The staff group had moved from 'blindness' to using their countertransference responses, their observations of themselves in relation to Carley, to trying to make sense of her experience. The next time I visited, the staff member who had been so in touch with Carley's helplessness, Claire, told me that the next time a resident had a visitor, she had sat with Carley and talked to her about how difficult it must be to see other people's visitors, but that she would be Carley's visitor today. She described how she said this, just as 'something to say' because she didn't want Carley to be on her own. She described how she had thought Carley wouldn't really understand as 'she didn't understand anything'. But to her surprise, Carley stopped poking at her eyes, and seemed to be looking at Claire with her one good eye. Claire said,

'I felt like she actually understood what I had said'. Claire started to spend more time actually talking to Carley. Over a period of time, the staff group reported that Carley was spending less of her time self-injuring, and that the staff group were feeling more positive towards her. Lydia Hartland-Rowe (2001) has described how detailed observations of people with severe learning disabilities can help us understand their internal worlds and can help with the process of 'linking up external and internal experience'. She describes how it is easy to be left with a feeling that it is 'too late' with this client group, but that this feeling may also reflect a person's experience of others not being able to bear thinking about them, as seems to have happened with Carley.

Communication considerations and settings

People with learning disabilities often have difficulty communicating. They may have physical disabilities that interfere with their ability to produce speech, or cognitive difficulties that have reduced their capacity to learn language. They may also have emotional difficulties that impinge on their ability to communicate, or more likely a combination of these difficulties.

It is also the case that people with lesser disabilities, including counsellors, can have difficulty hearing and listening to the communications of people with learning disabilities. This is not just a factor of attending to difficult speech, but in *really listening* to the experience of disability. It can be painful to be properly in touch with a person's experiences and distress. It may be easier not to really hear or listen. Ferenczi (1929) described how people with disabilities are receptacles or buckets for projections of society's disabilities. It is less painful to split off, and to project one's own weaknesses into people who are visibly less able. In really listening to people who are less able, we may be forced to take back our negative projections, or to own the weaker aspects of ourselves.

In trying to communicate, we may also have to compete with possible secondary handicaps that may be utilised by the client. Many clients have developed defensive strategies of hiding their negative emotions, their anger, distress and aggression, in order to make themselves more acceptable to others. So, in opening ourselves up to trying to hear the experience of people with disabilities, we may be acting against powerful structures and defences. This adds to the difficulty in this work. Communication is about listening, observing, trying to understand and name difficult emotions and processes. Even with all these obstacles, it is not impossible. Counselling is not just about language and words, but about understanding. When responding to a new-born baby's crying and distress, one talks to, comforts and holds the baby. We know that babies cannot cognitively understand the words that are being said, but they still seem to be comforted or interested in listening, watching the speaker's face and experiencing their tone of voice. We could use this analogy in counselling adults with learning disabilities. They may not always understand the spoken words, but they may well feel understood or held by the meaning conveyed in the words. Use of tone of voice and posture can also contribute to understanding. Alvarez (1992) has written about the use of tone and rhythm when working with autistic and very disturbed children. Mirroring or following a client's verbalisations can add to their sense of being thought about. This may mean being more active and physical than one would be in working with adults that do not have disabilities. It perhaps has greater parallels in the therapeutic work with children, where therapists often have to be flexible in following the child's lead, both physically and verbally in order to make a connection with the child at their developmental level.

With clients who do have speech, the use of language needs careful consideration. People with learning disabilities may need reflections, observations and interpretations to be made in a way that can be understood, with language carefully chosen and tested out. Parsons and Upson (1986) describe how concretely comments or interpretations can be received, and they suggest making explicit the difference between 'doing something' and 'feeling something', so for example one might need to say 'you worry something bad might happen to your mother, your feelings *will not make* something bad happen, but sometimes it *feels* like it will' in order for the client not to feel the counsellor was saying they were the cause of 'something bad'.

In order to provide the most conducive environment for effective communication to take place, there are a number of technical considerations, such as who should be invited to the first appointment and who should be written to regarding the appointment, especially when the client may not be able to read. Thought needs to go into how the client will travel to the clinic and get to the therapy room itself, especially if they have physical disabilities.

Although some flexibility may be needed, some 'rules' for structure and consistency should be adhered to. So, for example, one should try to keep to the same therapy room for all appointments, the same time and day for sessions, even for assessment appointments if possible. This helps the client feel contained and safe in the environment, reduces anxiety and enables transferences to be elicited more freely. Kahr (1997) makes several recommendations when setting up therapy with people with learning disabilities. Firstly, he highlights the importance of supervision and suggests that, where feasible, the process of supervision is started before the client is first seen, in order to be able to have an opportunity to think through reactions to the referral. Secondly, he recommends that, if an escorting arrangement is necessary, it should be established clearly from the outset. Thirdly, a consistent escort should be identified, and if this is not possible, the escorts need to be drawn from a consistent bank. He stresses the importance of both the escort and the therapist being accurate with their time keeping, in order to reduce anxiety and to demonstrate reliability and dependability. With these considerations taken into account, the structure is in place for an individual assessment to take place, so that a client's response to therapeutic contact, and one's own response to the client can be considered.

Evaluating a client's response to the assessment

A central aim of assessment for counselling is to explore a client's motivation, their willingness to form a therapeutic relationship and their ability to access and express feelings within this environment. In order to focus on these factors, we shall return to Louise, who was mentioned at the beginning of this chapter, to consider some formulations and hypotheses about her current difficulties. Formulations are necessary to guide the assessor towards appropriate reflections and interpretations. It is the client's responses to these interpretations that give an indication of their ability to use counselling.

Louise was referred because her social worker was concerned about her unusual mood swings. Louise and her mother attended the first assessment appointment. In this meeting I heard about the very difficult and painful circumstances of Louise's birth from her mother. Louise herself talked very little. She presented as a well-built young woman. She had an oval shaped face with attractive eyes. She seemed to avoid direct eye contact, instead looking at me through the corners of her eyes or sideways through her hair. She had long brown hair which hung like curtains around her face and behind which she seemed to retreat when things appeared more difficult for her to hear. She sat very close to her mother and seemed to need her mother's permission and reassurance to talk, looking to her mother whenever spoken to. Her mother, Mrs Clark, was also a well-built woman. She was in her fifties and presented emotionally as a flat, distant woman. She made no mention of Louise's father until asked directly, when she said that he had never really taken much interest in Louise's upbringing, he had left it mostly to her. She talked about how he worked long hours as a city accountant and had done so for many years. She added in an offhand tone that she wasn't even sure that she had mentioned this appointment to him.

The information gleaned so far, raised many questions, particularly about Mrs Clark's response to Louise's birth, and the difficult time she had following this. She described feeling isolated, miserable and exhausted, and it seems likely that she experienced depression following Louise's birth. It also seemed she was currently depressed, her affect was flat and distant. There were also questions to be considered about Louise and Mrs Clark's relationship in the light of both Louise's early days and her mother's current state. Did their early interactions have any impact on Louise's cognitive or emotional development? What was the impact on Louise now of her relationship with her mother? What was the impact on Louise of her parents' relationship and vice versa? There were many more questions than answers. However, we are now starting to gain information from which we can make tentative hypotheses.

In the last chapter we considered Klein, Bion and Winnicott's ideas about the importance of early relationships on both personality and cognitive development. Klein (1926) identified the importance of the infant's relationship with its mother. She hypothesised that an infant is born with an innate drive to make relationships. This hypothesis has to some extent been borne out by the work of Stern (1985) and Trevarthen (1976), who focused their research on the importance of lively and sensitive social relatedness between infants and carers from birth onwards.

Trevarthen (1976) explored what can happen when an infant's cues are not picked up on, or are responded to in an unusual or unpredictable way. It is possible that this can happen when a parent is not able to respond in the most positive way, perhaps because of events that have occurred in their own lives, or their own states of mind. If a parent does not respond in the way the infant expects or needs, the infant may not feel understood, or in Bion's terms, contained. This is bound to happen at times during all infants' early months, and most infants have enough experience of being understood and contained for this not to matter, or for difficult experiences to be integrated in a more useful way.

Bion (1962) described how, when an infant's experiences of being contained have on the whole been adequate, then experiences of frustration or needs not being met can force a *preconception* (Bion's term) of an idea into a thought. In other words, Bion hypothesised that the mental apparatus for independent thought is innate, but that in order for it to be used effectively, an infant must first have positive experiences of having others think for him or her, just as an infant needs to hear speech and be talked to, in order for language to develop. Some degree of frustration is important for development, but too much can hinder it.

In Louise's case, it may be that she has some organic brain damage, but it is also possible that she is experiencing some emotional difficulties that impede her to learn and develop further. We know that when Louise was very small her mother found it difficult to respond to her needy infant in a containing way. The combination of her low mood and Louise's special needs may have been too much for her to cope with. This mismatch may have had consequences for Louise's cognitive and emotional development. From a cognitive perspective, Louise may have found it difficult to develop her own ability to think, to connect isolated thoughts up into the process of thinking, if her early experience was that being thought about was difficult. From an emotional and personality perspective, Louise may have introjected, amongst other objects, an experience of her needs not being met, of a distant carer, and a need to be more difficult or distressed in order to get her needs recognised and met. This might go some way in explaining why at a point of transition, at a more stressful time, Louise's behaviour deteriorated. It may also partly explain Louise's difficulties in thinking, and how she and her mother have become so 'stuck' together. We have no direct evidence other than her mother's report that this is the case. However, as a starting hypothesis, it gives us some possibilities of thinking about Louise and her mother's difficulties. It also provides a structure for thinking about her treatment. If Louise internalised early difficult experiences that have had a persistent effect on subsequent relationships throughout her life, then the experience of counselling, of being thought about and understood, might be helpful to her.

When Louise as her mother has meet the counsellor, the counsellor had such a strong sense of Louise's anxiety that she felt able to comment on this their first meeting. She said that 'there seemed to be such a lot of worry and fear around, about coming to talk to someone about the difficulties Louise was having'. The counsellor wondered out loud if the possible move to college was causing Louise distress, making her feel more like a needy little girl than an adult. Perhaps there was also a worry about what might happen to her mother if Louise took another step towards growing up. Instead of looking to her mother, Louise looked directly at the therapist and nodded, with a look of relief in her eyes.

The aim of this assessment was both to develop some ideas about the origin of Louise's difficulties and to think about the viability of counselling. It seemed there was some evidence that a counselling approach could be appropriate for Louise's difficulties, as she was able to think about her feelings and respond to an interpretation. However, a major concern was that Louise seemed unable to participate in the assessment without her mother, while her mother tended to be disconnected from the process. It seemed that they were concretely demonstrating in the assessment some of their central difficulties in separating in a constructive way. In order to more fully explore Louise's ability to respond to a psychodynamic approach, it was likely that Louise and her mother would need to be seen separately. It could be argued that it might have been helpful to work with the family together, but it was felt that it was important to foster Louise's developing independence as an adult. When the plan to meet with them separately was proposed to Louise and her mother, it seemed to elicit a sense of both anxiety and relief that was so acute the therapist experienced it very strongly. We therefore organised for a colleague to meet with Louise's mother at the same time as Louise was seen for individual assessment.

SUMMARY

- One kind of assessment is a formal process of evaluating a client's ability to use counselling. However, assessment can also be considered as an evaluative state of mind, whereby thoughtful curiosity is maintained throughout all kinds of interactions with clients, whatever the relationship or setting.
- Completing formal assessments requires the gathering of an accurate history and evaluating the client's ability to form a working relationship; to use reflections and interpretations; and to think about, or be in touch with, their feelings.
- Assessment relies on the process of *observation*, not just of observable behaviours, but of the states of mind that accompany them, both in the client and in oneself. Therefore an understanding of one's own emotional responses and internal world is vital in making a helpful assessment of a client's object relations.
- In formal assessments, the context and setting needs proper consideration. How the client will be supported in getting to the counsellor needs to be thought about, as well as the consistency and suitability of the counselling setting. This consideration must include the timings of appointments, length of sessions and physical environment.
- In the room with the client, the assessment will be focused on

what they make of being with the counsellor, how they communicate, and how open they are to the counsellor's communications. Supervision and personal therapy can be extremely helpful in the process of understanding the unique relationship created between a client and counsellor.

4

FROM INFANCY TO OLD AGE: THINKING ABOUT LIFE STAGES

It is not unusual for referrers to be at a loss as to why behavioural or psychological problems have developed for clients at a particular point in time. Similarly it is often the case that everyday events are not considered relevant, meaningful or significant when trying to ascertain what is making a person feel or behave differently. Events that might seem irrelevant to others might in fact hold great importance to the person being assessed or treated. This is particularly true of events that bring into focus issues of loss, difference or absence.

CASE EXAMPLE: Brian

Brian, a 33-year-old man, was referred for counselling by his GP for aggressive outbursts. The referral stated that Brian had recently started to 'randomly shout and rant', interspersed with times when he became uncharacteristically withdrawn. His family and the local professional network were at a loss to know what might have provoked this behaviour in Brian, who was usually calm and outgoing.

Brian has mild learning disabilities and lives at home with his elderly mother. He has three siblings, a twin sister and two older brothers. His brothers are married and each has two children. His twin sister married last year and is now pregnant. Because his brothers and sisters left home several years ago, no-one in Brian's immediate family or network made any connection between his sister's pregnancy and Brian's distress. In the assessment for counselling, Brian presented as a slightly clumsy, but friendly, man who was keen to talk about himself and ask questions of the counsellor, such as where she lived, what she did in her spare time, and what car she drove. In the transference, these questions did not feel particularly intrusive, more like a curiosity about how he and she could link up, or make some kind of a relationship. When Brian started asking if she had children, the counsellor had a very different sense of being intruded upon. She felt quite anxious about how to manage her feelings and responses to Brian's repetitive, and increasingly obsessional, questioning. It was only in supervision, when describing Brian's background to the supervisor, that the counsellor was able to make a link between Brian's questions about children and the fact that his twin sister was shortly to have a baby. It became possible to think about what Brian's twin sister's pregnancy might have stirred up for him.

The therapist's thinking about Brian's experience seemed to enable Brian himself to become more able to think about the feelings of loss he was experiencing. Not only was he unlikely to parent children himself, but his feelings about being the damaged twin were reawakened: 'Even if someone did want to have a baby with me, it would probably be thick like me too'. Brian's behaviour started to improve gradually as he became more able to think about his feelings in relation to his sexuality, damage and loss of what might have been.

The last few decades have brought enormous changes in the way that people with learning disabilities have been viewed and treated. Following ideological developments such as Normalisation and legislative changes such as the 1990 Community Care Act the more recent emphasis on Clinical Governance leading to the development of the Care Programme Approach (DoH, 1999), social attitudes to the care and provision for people with learning disabilities have changed. People with learning disabilities are now more likely to live independently from their families, they are more likely to live in small 'family sized' homes (with live-in carers), and to be encouraged to participate in activities outside of their home such as work experience and day centres. Meaningful employment is more likely to be obtainable with the help of advocacy services such as People First, which provide support where necessary with employers.

These changes, combined with the medical developments that have ensured longer lives, and greater retention of physical independence (through aids where necessary), mean that people with disabilities have been facing different kinds of stressors over the last few decades. It is no longer the case that people with learning disabilities are seen to have static or life-long needs. In this chapter we will look more closely at issues that can arise at different life stages, such as leaving school, adolescence, moving home, siblings starting families, making relationships, taking up paid employment or growing old.

Families and a life cycle perspective

Pauline Boss has written, from a systemic perspective, about the process of *ambiguous loss*, where a family member may be physically present, but psychologically absent (Boss, 1991). She relates this idea to situations such as dementia or chronic drug abuse, but the impact of what she describes could be related to the unexpected birth of a child with a disability. Boss describes how this ambiguity (a loss, yet still the presence) can lead to helplessness, depression and conflict within families. She notes that when the ambiguity persists over time, it can block cognition as well as the emotional and behavioural responses that aid recovery. She describes the importance of helping families to reorganise themselves around the ambiguity, by challenging their perceptions and readjusting their expectations. She recommends that this is best done with all of the family present. Different members of the family can be at different points of adjustment at any one time, and this needs to be taken into consideration when working with whole families.

Similarly, Goldberg *et al.* (1995) document the recurrence of grief throughout the life cycle of a person with learning disabilities, and how this can impede the transitions between life stages, such as leaving home. They also recommend family work to evolve and develop hypotheses with the family about the current difficulties.

CASE EXAMPLE: Emma

Emma, aged 29, was referred for counselling by her GP, as she had reported to her family feeling depressed. Emma had a mild learning disability, of unknown cause, which was never really diagnosed, instead she was referred to as developmentally delayed, then 'statemented', or 'behind'. In her initial counselling session Emma spent the whole meeting complaining about her parents trying to make her go to college saying 'they just don't understand, you need to see them really'. Emma was an only child who lived at home with her obviously caring parents; however, it became apparent quickly that she found their interest in her life restrictive. The counsellor agreed to meet Emma together with her parents. At this meeting her parents talked about their difficulty in knowing how much to encourage Emma, as they did not really understand what was 'wrong' with her. They talked movingly about their struggles to try and find a reason for Emma's difficulties, and the impact this had on them as a couple, always focused on Emma. The counsellor experienced the family as still focused on past events and how they tell they had been treated by various professionals. It felt as if they found if difficult to move on or recognise Emma as an independent adult. Emma watched her parents carefully as they talked and she was able to say 'it doesn't really matter what is wrong with my brain, I am still me'. Following several meetings together, the family talked about being less preocupied with the past, and more able to think together about Emma's wishes and needs.

Birth and the early days

Although this is a book about working with adults, it is very difficult to consider psychological and relationship difficulties in any population, including that of people with learning disabilities, without recourse to a person's childhood. This is because, according to the work of clinicians such as Freud, Klein, Lacan and Bion, our earliest relationships influence what we bring to, and how we perceive, subsequent relationships or interactions throughout our lives. Our earliest ways of dealing with discomfort, conflict and distress can organise both our internal representations (objects) and our defence strategies from then on. This is why so much space has been devoted in this text to these early relationships.

There is a large literature on the impact on parents of the birth of a child with disabilities, which tends to draw parallels with the literature on bereavement. The birth of a baby with an obvious disability can be a shock and a disappointment. Bicknell (1983) likens parents' responses to those of grief, suggesting that stages need to be gone through in order to make an adjustment to the child with a disability. Other writers have likened the experience to that of a trauma. Korff-Sausse (1999) comments that many new parents of disabled children do not seem to have the capacity for the symbolisation that is necessary for mourning, that is, they are not able to put something in the place of the 'lost' object. She argues that this would explain why grief reoccurs, like trauma, with such intensity at key points in the person's life; the process of mourning is never complete.

There is evidence that recognising disability in one's child can be an extremely distressing experience. This distress occurs at a time when the infant is at his most needy. He or she will need their carers, their mother and father, to be open and available to his or her own distress and full range of other feelings. Depression and grief in the mother or father can make it difficult for them to be totally available to recognise and respond to the infant's distress. Stern (1995) describes the 'motherhood constellation', whereby a mother is supported by her mother and partner in the demanding job of being able to be available to the infant's often distressing projections. Grandparents and fathers are just as likely to have difficulty with an unexpected diagnosis, and therefore may not be as available at this time as the mother needs them to be.

During pregnancy, it is normal for a mother to have hopes, dreams and fantasies about her unborn baby (Raphael-Leff, 1993). When her child is born with an obvious defect, it can have a deep impact on the mother's ability to recognise, think about and contain the infant's distress. Because of the vulnerable state induced, for example, after a diagnosis or recognisable damage at birth, the mother may experience the infant's projections as unbearable confirmation of a terrible sense of damage. One way of dealing with this is to leave or reject the baby totally, as can be the case when children are placed for adoption. Depending on the way the infant managed his or her feelings at this time and the internal objects that were created, this process can be repeated throughout life. As an adult, the person may go on to have significant difficulty in maintaining relationships; in therapeutic relationships the counsellor may be rejected (for example, the client may not turn up for sessions) or by behaving in such a way that the counsellor wants to get rid of them, for example by behaving in a violent or disgusting way.

De Groef (1999) developed Freud's ideas about the narcissistic impulses associated with having children (Freud, 1914), when he describes how having children is part of a process of extending oneself. Yet the child becomes a reality through the birth, and is visibly *not* part of oneself, so all parents need to do some degree of mourning. A child born with disabilities is an acute narcissistic injury, an insult to one's extension. De Groef suggests that it is for this reason that people with disabilities are viewed either as angels on earth, fallen angels or devils. It feels too painful to view them as normal people because of the narcissistic injury this implies.

There are also potential difficulties in the containment structure that originate from the infant. For example, the infant's early distressful projections may be especially intense if their cognitive ability is organically impaired, or if they have a physical disability that impedes their ability to make optimum use of any caring environment that is available to them. According to Bion (1967) an infant's own aggressive impulses may distort the complicated interplay between infants and carers in an unhelpful way. That is to say that carers alone are not responsible for the internalised objects, and that an infant's constitutional make up is also important, in particular the infant's capacity to tolerate frustration.

Managing separation and independence

Processes that hinder the development of separation may be functional for very young infants, protecting both the child and his or her parents from premature and possibly damaging separations. As the child grows, however, an over close relationship can create difficulties for both the child and the parent in tolerating normal developmental separation. In order to tolerate separateness, the person with disabilities has to recognise and accept his or her own disabilities and imperfections. Parents may feel that it would be too difficult and painful for the child if they did allow them to experience the full extent of their disabilities. Remaining overly close can protect both the parents and child from having to experience the full impact of any damage.

One way families can manage their feelings about their child's disability is to pretend it doesn't exist, to deny it. For example, in child services it is not uncommon for parents to 'shop' around for a more preferable diagnosis, or to over-organise speech or physiotherapy with the aim of 'taking away' the disabilities. This can be seen as a manic denial of disability, treatment as if normal, or an idealisation of disability so the child is seen as a blessing or special gift. Parents' (and society's) denial can go two different ways along this continuum. It can make it difficult for the person with the disability to openly acknowledge any disability when he or she is aware of it and wants help, while at the other end of the spectrum the person may introject a complete denial of any disability, so that help cannot be asked for or acknowledged when it is needed.

CASE EXAMPLE: Irene

Irene is a nineteen-year-old woman with mild learning disabilities, who was referred for counselling by her social worker because of difficulties in her work experience placements. Irene is on her third placement, the first two having broken down because Irene was unable to take instructions from her employers, choosing instead to argue with and criticise them. Irene agreed to the referral, saying that it would help her 'prove' that she was right and they were wrong.

Irene is an only child, living at home with her parents. She attended mainstream school, but struggled enormously to keep up. She was extremely demanding and took up a lot of teaching time. At a review it was suggested that she transfer to a special school. Both Irene and her mother were outraged at this suggestion, and insisted that she continue in mainstream education. On leaving school, Irene's social worker found her a work experience placement in an office. She found this very difficult as she was expected to help with office tasks such as photocopying and filing. Irene complained bitterly about this, insisting she should be, at the very least, typing. However, when the office manager relented and let her take on more complicated tasks, she couldn't cope and Irene blamed the manager for her difficulties. When this placement broke down she was moved to a catering placement where once again the same process occurred. Irene was unable to manage even simple tasks, so the placement reorganised her time so that she would experience more successes. Irene was furious, saying she was being given tasks that were 'for stupid people', and 'not for me'. When this placement finally broke down, Irene and her mother met with, and convinced, her social worker that it was the placements themselves that had been the problem; staff had put Irene down and 'did not give me a chance'. The social worker organised for her to take up a placement in a hairdressers as an apprentice, but on the proviso that she attend a clinic for counselling, to which she agreed. On the placement, Irene immediately got into disputes with the manager, because she was not allowed to cut clients' hair.

When Irene attended her first meeting at the clinic, she brought her mother with her. They presented a unified front, describing how difficult the managers on the placements had been, and how unprepared they were to give Irene a chance. Not once did either of them talk about Irene's limitations. When Irene was seen on her own, she continued to be angry about the way she 'had been treated'. She talked about how the other apprentices were being trained in cutting hair, but they just wanted her to make tea and sweep up. It felt to the counsellor like Irene's mother was still in the room, her dominance was so tangible. Irene seemed to have introjected her mother's difficulty with acknowledging Irene's learning disabilities, and she seemed unable to tolerate any mention of disability or to acknowledge the need for any help. The counsellor initially felt very stuck and sympathetic to Irene, whom she agreed had been mistreated. However, when the counsellor discussed this

Continued

impasse with a colleague, the colleague pointed out that the counsellor seemed to have been caught up in Irene and her mother's projections; she was seeing herself as unable and failing, because she felt she couldn't help. Armed with this different kind of understanding, the next time Irene made her feel incompetent, she commented that it seemed as if Irene was so angry with everyone else that it made it feel difficult and humiliating to ask for help when she felt stuck. Irene disagreed with this comment, but then was able to verbalise a disagreement with her mother about what she wanted to do. Irene described how she had always enjoyed gardening, and she hoped to get a placement with the local gardening company. Her mother had said no, gardening was 'below her'. Irene talked with pleasure about what she had done in her own corner of the family garden, but then commented 'perhaps my mother is right, its not for me. Anyway I probably wouldn't be any good at it'. It seemed as if Irene had become so identified with her mother's projections that she behaved as if she was her mother at times. This, combined with her harsh *super-ego* (the internalised 'parental' objects that tend to be more critical and judgmental) that demanded perfection seemed to limit her abilities even further. Once Irene's counsellor was able to separate herself from these harsh projections of failure, she was able to offer Irene the possibility of a different way of thinking.

As children grow and develop into adolescents and then adults there are several stages or processes they need to go through in order to function independently and appropriately as adults. However, the disability itself, and their own and their family's feelings regarding the disability can make these stages much more difficult to pass through successfully. These 'stages' or processes include oedipal developments, adolescence, and successfully managing the independence that adulthood confers.

It is also important to recognise that these stages are not necessarily age specific, and that sometimes, through the process of counselling or due to life events, adults can become more in touch with infantile and adolescent feelings and experiences. If processes in adolescence or indeed infancy have not been adequately resolved or negotiated, then the emotional disturbances from these periods of life that have been internalised can have an ongoing impact. An adult who did not have adequate containing experiences as an infant is likely to struggle as an adult with all relationships. An adolescent who was not enabled to develop autonomy is likely to continue to be dependent in adulthood. Through the course of counselling, it is possible that clients will move between infantile, adolescent and adult ways of relating to, and experiencing, the relationship with the counsellor, and this can enable real thinking in the 'here and now' about these issues. An understanding of emotional development and emotional milestones in childhood and adolescence is therefore essential to the counsellor in this work.

Sexual development and the Oedipus complex

The development of sexuality starts very early in life, as infants begin to discover that their feelings towards each parent fluctuate and differ. Parents are normally a child's first 'love object' and the feelings they have about each parent separately, and their growing understanding about their parents' own relationship can create very powerful emotions that form the basis of our ability to relate to people of the same and of different genders. Difficulties in early sexual development and an individual's ability to successfully integrate anxieties generated by having to share loved ones with others, are likely to have a significant impact on future relationships. Early internal negotiations around the anxiety generated by having more than one loved object cumulate in the development of what is famously known as the Oedipus complex. The Oedipus complex was defined by Freud in 1918 as 'the root of all neuroses'. He saw this as a process that occurs within a specific stage of development that takes place in all infants between the ages of three and five. He described how this stage is characterised by an infant's sexual feelings and desires, which he or she attempts to manage, by directing them towards his or her parents. He described how directing these feelings towards others can lead to anxieties and fears, such as castration anxiety in boys and penis envy in girls. Klein's observational studies gave her a different perspective on this

71

theory, and she modified Freud's ideas significantly (Klein, 1928). Like all her theorising, she based her ideas on watching children at play. In common with Freud, she observed how children develop identifications with each parent, and she also noted the simple form of the Oedipus couple, a hatred for one parent and a love of the other, in the children she studied. However, she also saw evidence of *oedipal phantasies* in much younger children, certainly before age three. She observed that sadistic and aggressive impulses were associated with these phantasies, which in turn resulted in great anxiety, fear and remorse. The child fears that his impulses will cause actual damage to his or her parents, and that his parents will retaliate against him.

In people with learning disabilities, these processes can be impeded at several levels. Sinason (1992) describes how Oedipal fantasies can feel very powerful, especially when a person continues to be dependent on their parent into adulthood. Marital breakdown is more likely when living with the stress and blame of a disability (Dale, 1995). Blame can be all the more acute when there is the reality of an inheritable genetic condition such as Fragile X syndrome. Physical dependency can also have an impact on a person's ability to manage their Oedipal phantasies, especially when physically intimate acts such as washing and bathing have to be done by a parent into adulthood. Often families manage this conflict by viewing their child as a helpless baby rather than a sexually developing adolescent or adult. Any effort to resist this perception can be very dangerous, eliciting negative feelings from carers. When a person with learning disabilities and his or her family allow the recognition of adulthood to occur, negative feelings about the disability may become more apparent, and with this, the uncomfortable feelings that it might be better all round if 'something happened' to the person. People with learning disabilities who make their sexuality and sexual needs known, by talking about them or openly masturbating can make other people feel both guilt and disgust. Sinason (1992) describes how one defence that people with learning disabilities can develop regarding their unmet sexual needs is a secondary handicap. All their feelings about their difference are projected on to other disabled people, who will never be 'good enough' as a sexual partner, and onto the relationship of love itself, so that this is experienced as a degraded sexuality.

CASE EXAMPLE: Aaron

Aaron is a twenty-five-year-old man who lives at home with his mother, Mrs Prout. Aaron has moderate learning disabilities and Down's Syndrome. He was referred for counselling by his GP because of panic attacks. Aaron is a short, stocky man who has the notable facial features of Downs Syndrome. Mrs Prout is also short and has a tired, worn-out look about her. They both attended the first assessment meeting because Mrs Prout said that Aaron couldn't manage without her, and that he had a panic attack when she suggested he talk to the counsellor on his own. Aaron has a wide vocabulary and talked openly in his mother's presence. They told the counsellor a sad story about how Mrs Prout had three miscarriages before Aaron was born, and that Mr Prout left home when Aaron was nearly two, following several episodes of domestic violence, to which Aaron was witness. Aaron said he didn't know his dad and did not have any contact with him. They also talked about how Mrs Prout had brought up Aaron on her own with very little support as her family lived at a great distance. In the last couple of years Mrs Prout had started a relationship with a man from her work, whom Aaron said he liked: 'Mike is my mate, we go to football together'. Mrs Prout said the relationship was in its early stages. Mr Price (Mike) also had adult children and they had no immediate plans to live together. Following the assessment Aaron started individual counselling. In his sessions he talked repetitively about his mother, all the activities they did together, how much she loved him, how much they were best friends. Aaron described his panic attacks as times when he couldn't breathe and he felt strongly that he just needed to get back to his home. He described how these attacks only happened outside of home, because at home his mother always managed to keep him calm. In the transference the counsellor felt the level of anxiety rising when Aaron talked about his mother, and at one point she said how worried Aaron seemed to be about his mother, and that perhaps he feared she might not really love him enough. Aaron denied this but his breathing quickened and he was clearly starting

Continued

to panic. He started to stroke the side of his head, and he managed to calm himself down. The counsellor commented on this, she wondered if Aaron's mother also comforted him in this way. Aaron thought about this and said that when he was little his mother looked after him very well. Aaron said 'she had to look after me well as my dad was a very bad man, you know he was bad, I looked after her too, I can look after her as well'. He started to panic, his breathing quickened and he started to cry, then left, running back to the waiting room where his mother was waiting for him. His counsellor was left feeling as if she had intruded into Aaron's relationship with his mother, almost as if she had criticised his mother. Aaron returned the next week saying he did not want the counsellor to talk about his dad like that. The counsellor pointed out that it was Aaron that had brought up his dad, but that she thought Aaron's dad was still very much alive in his mind. Aaron started to sob, saying in a confused jumbled way that his dad didn't want him because he was disabled but that he had made his dad go away because he was bad and that now his mum was going to leave him because he was disabled and now she had Mike not him. Aaron was clearly caught up in his feelings that related back to his father's departure and his feeling that he had both taken his father's place, and at the same time that he could never take his father's place because of his disability; his mother didn't love him because of his disability. The counsellor was then able slowly to tease out some of these issues, and to help Aaron see that his panic attacks might be related both to his fear of losing his mother and his guilt and fear about driving his father away.

Sinason (1992) has suggested that for boys the oedipal fantasy of marrying your mother and killing off your father can have an extra dimension, they can marry their mother by creating an exclusive dependent relationship, and the father is killed off by the presence of handicap. In Aaron's mind this fantasy had been given real life. It appears that Aaron had not yet helpfully negotiated important aspects of his sexual and emotional development, and that this was continuing to have repercussions in his adult life.

Pre-adolescence

The period of time before puberty, but after the intense period of development in the pre-school years is sometimes known as 'the latency years'. This is owing to Freud's belief that the real focus of this time was the consolidation of the sexuality developing in the very turbulent early years. However, whilst contemporary theorists would agree that sexual development is less of an immediate focus during this period, they would argue that other very important developments are occurring, and that this period of time is by no means a static time in development. The emotional turmoil of an infant's early years do need to be fully assimilated and generally this period can be a calmer time emotionally, where the distinction between the self and internal objects becomes more defined. However, important developments are taking place in other aspects of the self, for example the development of autonomy, intellectual and social functioning (Alvarez, 1989). When there have been early difficulties, especially with the processes of projective identification (when parts of the self are split off and projected into an external object, but then the external object is experienced as being controlled by and identified with the projections), projection and introjection, this is a time where these difficulties can become more entrenched and fixed. This can be seen when an older child does not appear to be developing the ability to become independent, to develop relationships outside of the family or to be making the most from their educational environment. They may find it difficult to tolerate frustration and anxiety; skills that tend to be built on during this time. Any lack of internal containment can impede emotional and intellectual development in an ongoing way. Early difficulties in containment and separation can thus become compounded during this stage of development.

Adolescence

Adolescence is generally seen as the time after puberty strikes, before adulthood is officially reached. It is characterised by a focus on developing adult sexuality, growing autonomy and independence. Sexuality and relationships need to be dealt with as puberty takes hold. Socially, the capacity for increasing intimate relationships with friends and eventually in the work place is developed. Not surprisingly these tasks can be hindered or impeded when learning disabilities are thrown into the equation. Adolescence can be a very difficult and distressing time for people with learning difficulties as they struggle with their growing awareness of their difference and how others view them. The struggle for independence when one is physically or socially dependent on others can be an uphill battle.

CASE EXAMPLE: Amy

Amy, a sixteen-year-old girl, has Smith–Magenis Syndrome with both moderate learning disabilities and unusual facial features; her eyes are widely spaced, and her whole face is notably flat. She was referred for counselling because of her school's concerns about her sexual behaviour. She was found half dressed in a stationery cupboard with a male at her special school, and she has been noted to kiss and touch other pupils and male staff 'inappropriately'. Initially a referral was made to the child protection team, as unusual sexual behaviour often indicates abuse, and a full investigation took place. Amy did not disclose abuse in the memorandum interview, and the investigation found no indication of any concerns at home. Amy lives at home with her parents and older sister. The family had co-operated fully with the investigation, her parents said that they were mortified by Amy's behaviour, as sexual matters had been avoided at home. Her parents thought that she did not need to know about sexual relationships as she would be unlikely to ever have one. Therefore the conclusion of the investigation was that Amy's behaviour was related to her struggle with puberty and adolescence. The family were referred for counselling, but her parents refused to participate, saying that they thought Amy would just 'grow out' of her 'childish' behaviour. Amy attended her sessions regularly, but the counsellor found it difficult to get a sense of her emotional state. Amy would bring objects from home to show the counsellor, such as school work, photographs and decorative treasures such as glass paperweights with stone animals inside, jewellery and glittery purses. The counsellor felt distracted by these treasures and commented that Amy wanted very much to make a friend of the counsellor, to share pleasure in these objects, but most importantly not to think about Amy's disability and how she was different. The counsellor felt very anxious about drawing attention to this, as Amy had worked so hard to keep the focus away from herself. However, Amy seemed relieved. She threw the necklace she was showing the counsellor on the floor and said 'Whatever I wear won't get me a boyfriend will it?' The counsellor gently said that Amy felt she needed to make herself look special with the jewellery, as she worried that she would not be good enough without it. This acknowledgement of Amy's distress of being different during adolescence when being 'one of the crowd' is so important, and one's perception about how one looks can feel dreadfully important, allowed Amy to use the counselling more effectively. Over the next few sessions she became furious with the counsellor 'I know you think I am ugly', and gradually was able to think about her more angry feelings towards her family for holding back her development. The counsellor was made aware of Amy's harsh self-judgement projected into the counsellor. Amy began to talk more openly about her sexuality and with this came an understanding that she did not need to allow others to abuse her in order to be liked. 'When Johnny kisses me I hate it because he tries to touch me and I don't like that, but when Phil kisses me, its good, he wants to hold my hand'. Amy seemed to be struggling with being a learning disabled adolescent who was not given permission to experiment with adolescent relationships because her parents denied she could ever understand about adult sexuality. This denial put her at risk of abuse, as can happen when there is an assumption that people with learning disabilities do not have or understand sexual feelings.

Relationships in adulthood

Defensive structures and methods of communication are normally well established by the time we reach adulthood, as dictated by our internal objects. For the 'non disabled' adult, reaching adulthood is an important milestone. It is associated with moving away from one's family of origin, living independently, making long-term relationships, starting families and taking up meaningful activities during the day such as employment or raising families. For the adult with learning disabilities there are often very different expectations, or more often than not, a lack of expectations. They are much more likely to leave home at a later age and to have accommodation arranged for them. They may have to go somewhere that has been planned for them, rather than having the same kinds of choices as other people. It is painful when siblings achieve more than they do: getting qualifications, girl or boyfriends, husbands or wives, jobs and homes of their own. As can be seen in the example of Brian at the beginning of this chapter, these absent life transitions can reawaken feelings of loss or insecurity throughout the life span. People with learning disabilities can and do form lasting marital relationships, although these tend to be in the minority. With ideological changes and service developments such as O'Brien's five accomplishments (O'Brien, 1987) and the principles of normalisation, attitudes towards the sexual lives of people with learning disabilities are gradually beginning to change.

There are now many texts acknowledging the rights of people with disabilities to have sexual relationships (Craft, 1994). There now exists a self support organisation (SPOD; Sexual Problems of the Disabled) providing support and advice. These developments are necessary and positive. However, there is still a very high incidence of sexual abuse towards people with learning disabilities, and there is often a fine line to tread in trying to ascertain whether a relationship is fully consensual on both sides (see examples in Craft, 1994). The impact of sexual abuse will be considered more fully in the next chapter.

Relationships with keyworkers

Adults with learning disabilities are also frequently faced with having to make relationships with people employed to help them such as social workers, residential social workers, and nurses. These relationships tend to be relatively short-lived, but full of emotional investment.

There is considerable literature on the numerous transitions that people with learning disabilities tend to have to make throughout their lifetime. The number of transitions are likely to be greater for people who were living in large-scale residential accommodation since the government legislative changes of community care. Even without a move from a large-scale residential hospital, people with disabilities can often experience a number of moves, from one residential home to another.

Less has been written about the regular changes in staff that people with learning disabilities have to contend with. Residential and day work with people with learning disabilities tends to be poorly paid and stressful, hence the high turnover of staff and high level of sick leave that is common. Mattison and Pistrang (2000) have looked in detail at the impact these frequent losses have on this client group, and on the workers in question. They focus in particular on keyworker relationships, which are created almost universally in residential settings. Mattison and Pistrang explore the range of feelings generated by the loss of a keyworking relationship for both clients and staff by qualitatively analysing interviews with both clients and keyworkers. This analysis has generated a number of themes. These included the range of ways in which clients viewed their relationship with their keyworker, such as experiencing the keyworker as being a provider, nurturer, companion and a provider of constancy. The range of ways staff saw their roles with their clients was slightly different including being a provider, a meaning maker, companion and a family to the client. Given this range of important roles it is not surprising that powerful feelings are evoked in both clients and staff when keyworkers leave their post (or no longer keywork the client). For clients the themes were:

- loss and grief
- helplessness
- acceptance
- acquiescence

Mattison and Pistrang (2000) describe how they were struck by the lack of expressed anger or envy in the clients' responses, although they described feeling powerless and excluded from any decision-making, and in some cases even from saying goodbye.

They hypothesise that this absence is caused by a denial of their feelings, an unconscious strategy to protect themselves from fully experiencing their disability and dependence.

For staff the feelings centred around:

- attachment and separation
- denial
- self devaluation

It is probably for the issues described above that keyworkers tend to leave in less than ideal circumstances, often leaving with little or no notice to the clients. Mattison and Pistrang describe how the sudden and abrupt staff departures create a sense of confusion, bewilderment and shock in the clients. Two themes that both keyworkers and clients referred to were the issues around whether to keep in touch or not and the ritualised goodbye pleasantries such as leaving parties.

What can be seen from this important study is that keyworkers leaving can stir up powerful feelings for clients. Obviously how a person manages loss will have a lot to do with how they have managed past significant losses. For the client who has experienced frequent or significant rejections, it would be hard not to experience a keyworker leaving as a personal rejection.

CASE EXAMPLE: Winston

In a consultation to a staff team, a particularly difficult client, Winston, was being discussed. Winston's keyworker, Elroy, said, 'I have had enough of him, he is demanding and he constantly creates petty arguments, he is too much to take'. Elroy talked about how the staff team had agreed to rotate the keyworking responsibility to Winston on a six monthly basis. The staff team moved on to think about Winston's background and said they did not know too much about his home life; his mother was a schizophrenic and there was no record of his father. Elroy said that he thought Winston had been brought up in a children's home after several failed attempts at fostering him. He did not know why the attempts had failed. The staff team described how Winston made them feel angry and hopeless, he was demanding and argumentative; 'too much to take'. When asked how they thought Winston felt about being moved from keyworker to keyworker, Elroy started by saying Winston did not seem to care, however another staff member pointed out that when Winston's last keyworker, Sandy, had left, Winston had become quite withdrawn and had gone through a period of encopresis and enuresis. We wondered about these symptoms, more typical of a young child than a twenty-four year old man, and Elroy commented that he wondered if it meant Winston felt infantalised by the loss. This led us to thinking how Winston may be experiencing each new loss as traumatically as his early losses, of family and home, and how each new loss might confirm his feelings of being worthless and 'shitty'. The next time I saw this staff group, Elroy described how he had started to feel differently about Winston, and he felt less willing to be pushed away by him. He had decided to persevere with working with Winston, but had asked for extra supervision to manage his feelings about Winston's difficult behaviour.

We can see how Elroy seemed to be organised into pushing Winston away by Winston's behaviour. Winston seemed to be projecting aspects of his internal 'rejecting' object into Elroy, an internalisation that may have taken place as a result of his early experiences. Sometimes it can be easier to distance oneself than to really think about difficult relationships with clients. However, through a process of thinking we can gain deeper understanding of the processes that can occur between ourselves and the clients we work closely with.

Growing older with a learning disability

As is the case in the general population, people with learning disabilities are living to older ages, and are experiencing the kinds of associated difficulties, including an increased dependency, reduced mobility and sensory decline. There is also an increased risk of dementia, and this is particularly the case for people with Down's Syndrome, whose risk rises significantly past the age of about 40 years. It is important to consider dementia as a possible cause for emotional difficulties in older adults and this needs to be borne in mind when making an assessment. However, becoming older can be associated with a range of emotional difficulties, as for example the transition into being a 'pensioner' is another milestone that can highlight losses throughout one's life. Older adults with learning disabilities are less likely to have close friends and family to depend on; it can be a very isolating experience as services become withdrawn as the person is no longer eligible for them. With increasing age, people with learning disabilities are also more likely to have had to deal with many losses of workers, and of deaths of people close to them.

CASE EXAMPLE: Ms Avery

Ms Avery is a sixty-six-year-old woman with a mild learning disability. She has lived in a small group home for the last thirty years, and until recently had attended a day centre for adults with learning disabilities three days a week. Her parents are both dead, her mother died when she was forty-eight and her father died four years later. In the last three years two other residents of the home have died, and she openly grieved their deaths, both of whom she has known for the majority of her life. Their rooms have been taken by two new residents whom Ms Avery seems to get on with, though she does not actively seek their company.

Recently Ms Avery started to behave in an odd way. She was found wandering in the streets at two o'clock in the morning with just her underwear on, and she has been quite forgetful, leaving her glasses in the fridge and in cereal packets. The home staff were concerned as one of the residents who died recently had suffered from dementia, so they referred Ms Avery to the local psychiatrist. The psychiatrist could find no evidence of dementia and he concluded that Ms Avery was slowly losing cognitive skills and that she was also depressed. He recommended the use of visual cues for memory in the house and he referred Ms Avery for counselling.

Ms Avery attended the first appointment in a seemingly cheerful mood, she smiled a lot and talked about how she was 'okay', there was nothing wrong with her and she didn't really need to come and 'talk to the nice lady'. She told her life story in a very bland matter-of-fact way with a fixed rather handicapped smile on her face. At the second meeting she continued as if there had not been a break, talking about all the things she does, the places she goes, so really she must be 'okay', and there was really 'no point in wasting the nice lady's time'. The counsellor found it hard to listen to Ms Avery's chatter, and instead found herself thinking about Ms Avery wandering around in the night in her underwear. This thought brought a wave of sadness over the counsellor and she found that Ms Avery had stopped talking and was looking at her rather intently and anxiously, with the same fixed smile. The counsellor said that although Ms Avery was saying that everything was okay, she wondered if Ms Avery was really quite worried that things were not really okay. The smile dropped. Ms Avery put her head in her hands, let out a tearless wail, and insisted on leaving. The counsellor was left with the sense that Ms Avery was terribly concerned about what people might think of her and the strain of keeping a happy face at times felt overwhelming. Ms Avery continued to come for counselling, and found ways of talking about the enormous sense of loss she felt at her parents' deaths, and more recently at her friend's illness and subsequent death. She was able to talk about her fears that she was 'not really myself, but somebody else', and the lack of control she felt about the arrangements made for her. Ms Avery lost the cheerful smile and became more obviously distressed, but staff felt they understood her behaviour and distress in a different kind of way.

SUMMARY

- The fact that people with learning disabilities have life cycles, with stages, such as adolescence and older age with associated feelings is often overlooked or minimised.

- Giving thought to a person's life stage, and the context of their family and friends can often help in the understanding of any difficulties they may present with.
- Difficulties can also be generated by the lack of events or life stages, for example not gaining separation at adolescence, not gaining meaningful employment or having children.
- The impact of having to make and lose significant relationships with workers, such as keyworkers, throughout one's life is often underestimated. It can be quite painful never to have the opportunity to choose how and when people come and go; this can stir up previous losses and separations in the process.

5

Consideration of Specific 'Presenting Problems' – How Can a Counselling Approach be of Use?

A range of identified or 'presenting problems' that are most frequently cited as 'reasons for referral' to learning disability mental health services are now considered. This will include a discussion about abuse, particularly the consequences of abuse experienced as a child, loss, bereavement, challenging behaviour, psychiatric diagnosis, and sensory impairments. Talking treatments for challenging behaviours tend to be neglected in favour of medical or behavioural approaches, because they are seen as conditions that have biological aspects. There is, however, a growing body of evidence that counselling can be of use for a wide range of presenting problems. We will start by looking at one of the most common referral reasons, that of abuse.

Abuse

Abuse towards people with learning disabilities is unfortunately very common, and can take many forms including physical, sexual, emotional, financial, neglect and discrimination (Emerson *et al.*, 2001). A recent study indicated that 23 per cent of people with learning disabilities have been physically abused and 47 per cent have experienced verbal abuse (Brown, 1999). Other studies suggested that up to 1400 new cases of sexual abuse towards adults with learning disabilities are occurring every year in the UK (Brown *et al.*, 1995, McCarthy and Thompson, 1997). These figures are shocking and disturbing, but perhaps not so surprising given the way in which people with learning disabilities are often thought of as different. This perceived difference allows a split between 'them and us', which can facilitate the development of negative projections. It is arguably easier to abuse people who are seen as less than human or different. People with learning disabilities can be extremely vulnerable, especially when they have physical disabilities, as they cannot physically resist or prevent abuse from occurring. Speech difficulties may make disclosure more difficult. There is evidence that prosecutions of offenders are less likely because people with learning disabilities are not considered to be good or reliable witnesses (Gunn, 1994).

Abuse of people with learning disabilities is now more openly recognised and acknowledged, although on an individual level it is still painful to think about or consider. Corbett, Cottis and Morris (1996) discuss the painful feelings that can be evoked when workers really allow themselves to recognise and think about the abuse their clients have suffered. They describe the importance of the process of 'being there', holding and containing the person's experience and providing the opportunity for a non-abusive attachment. If the counsellor has the capacity to think about, and to tolerate, the pain and reality of people's circumstances, then the client is more like to be able to *introject* (to take in) this capacity.

Corbett *et al.* (1996) using their experience from setting up RESPOND, a London-based service that works specifically with people with learning disabilities who have been sexually abused, have described the important aspects of a therapeutic relationship where sexual abuse is its focus. The therapeutic tasks that they identify are: *witnessing, protesting* and *nurturing*. By witnessing they mean bearing to hear or think about the client's experiences. Protesting is primarily the process whereby there is a clear acknowledgement that abuse is wrong, and that this conviction is not silenced or hidden. Nurturing is the provision of a safe and secure new relationship. They describe how their work has been influenced by the literature on attachment and loss; the experience of sexual abuse can result in a profound sense of loss. Often the pattern of responses following a disclosure of abuse is similar to those following a bereavement, so that denial, anger, weeping and numbness are all common responses. These responses cathect much of the pain, and having someone who can survive a person's anger and distress may help in the process of restoring an equilibrium where good feelings can be experienced in spite of the loss.

CASE EXAMPLE: Janice

Janice, a twenty-two-year-old woman who has severe and profound learning disabilities was referred for counselling following deterioration in her behaviour. She has lived in care since she was seven years old. The referrer, the manager of her home, stated that Janice has been touching her genitals and masturbating inappropriately. Before Janice was seen, the counsellor met with the manager of the home who explained that Janice had recently started to masturbate in public whilst on trips out. Janice is wheelchair bound and has very little language, and it quickly transpired that there are very few places that are 'private' for Janice, however the staff group have been intent on trying to teach her that she can masturbate only in her room or the bathroom. The manager said that it is hard to make Janice understand this, but they keep trying because her behaviour is making everyone feel uncomfortable.

Janice was seen for an assessment for counselling. A female member of staff from the home brought Janice to the clinic, and took her to the therapy room, leaving her with the counsellor, without any comment to Janice. The counsellor felt shocked at the lack of contact between Janice and the worker. Janice sat slouched silently and passively in her wheelchair, avoiding eye contact with the counsellor. The counsellor talked to Janice about how strange and different it might feel coming to the clinic, but Janice did not respond, and the counsellor felt strongly that Janice was distrustful of her. She commented on how difficult it felt for Janice to be here, and how she had a sense that Janice found it difficult to think anyone might be able to help her, or even to be interested in her feelings. Janice

Continued

looked directly at the counsellor and lifted up her skirt and began to masturbate. The counsellor felt shocked and overwhelmed by this behaviour; she wanted to turn away and to get away. Aware of these feelings, she talked about how she had a sense that Janice wanted her to know something shocking, that Janice was trying to communicate something awful, but perhaps she felt the counsellor might just turn away from her. Janice mumbled something under her breath that sounded like 'Miles'. The counsellor asked if she said 'Miles' and Janice smiled defiantly and sat more upright in her wheelchair. The counsellor said that she understood from Janice that someone called Miles made her feel uncomfortable and she wanted to get away. The counsellor told Janice that what she had said was very serious, and that she would have to talk to a social worker about it. Janice seemed to relax, she nodded in agreement and then turned her face away, hiding her expression.

The counsellor learnt that Miles was a worker in the day centre that Janice attended and a full investigation took place. It became clear that Miles had been sexually abusing a number of the less able day centre users over a long period of time, and he was eventually prosecuted.

Janice's behaviour was a painful communication about her experience, and she had the courage to let others know what was happening to her. However, it took courage to hear and think about the communication, as the counsellor felt strongly that she too wanted to ignore the meaning, to turn away from the communication. She was however able to stay with Janice and to 'think the unthinkable'. Janice went on to attend weekly counselling for two years, during which the full extent of the damage she felt by her experience became more apparent.

It is not uncommon for people who have experienced abuse to develop abusive behaviours themselves. Having been abused in childhood is a positive risk factor in developing abusive behaviour, especially for men (Glasser et al., 2001). When it is suspected that a person may be abusing other people, this first needs to be properly assessed and managed through appropriate risk assessments and treatment. Only when a clear management plan is in place can counselling treatments be helpfully utilised.

CASE EXAMPLE: Mark

Mark is a thirty-one-year-old man with a moderate learning disability who has been arrested for exposing himself to young children on several occasions. On one occasion he attempted to rape a ten-year old boy. Mark has been detained under the Mental Health Act and he lives in a secure unit. As part of the treatment programme he attends regular weekly counselling.

Mark has a history of being abused and neglected as a child. He was placed in care when he was thirteen years old, as his mother appeared to be unable to look after him, he rarely attended school and his behaviour was disruptive when he did. His mother's brother sexually abused Mark over a period of four years from when he was six to ten, the abuse stopping when his uncle went to prison for similar offences to his own children.

Mark has been attending counselling for the last year, and during this time he has been able to think about his own history of abuse. It has been very painful for him to talk about what happened to him, but also very important as, with increasing insight, he has developed some capacity for remorse about his behaviour. Counselling has enabled Mark to make some links between his own behaviour and his earlier experiences. The work has been long and slow, though on occasions when the counsellor has been able to stick with the more difficult feelings for long periods of time, then Mark has been able to make real connections between his past experiences and his behaviour. An example is given with the extract from a therapy session below.

Mark continued to complain about how the staff were treating him, how he never got as much attention as other residents, he moaned that they even got more food than he did. The counsellor voiced his thoughts about Mark's feelings that he was not getting enough from the therapy, that he seemed to be experiencing the counsellor as withholding. Mark sat silently for some time then said 'I have been thinking about touching boys again' the counsellor wondered about the relationship between Mark's feelings of neglect and his wish to abuse, but said nothing. Mark started to sob, saying, 'I just wanted him (the child he had abused) to like me'.

It seemed as if the counsellor's thoughts, even though not verbally expressed, allowed Mark to be able to develop his own thoughts; the process of staying with Mark and providing a containing, thoughtful mind facilitated Mark's emotional development. Mark seemed more able to find a space in his own mind for reflection on his suffering, part of the process of tolerating his feelings rather than *acting them out* (defensively acting his phantasies out outside of counselling sessions). The counsellor also had regular detailed supervision about his work, which helped him to identify and think about his more difficult responses to Mark. Working with abuse can elicit a range of powerful feelings that may relate to our own backgrounds and experiences. Corbett *et al.* (1996) make the point of the necessity of good supervision when working in this area. Workers need to have their own feelings contained. When working with abuse it is easy to become overwhelmed, and without a space for reflection the worker may manage the feelings generated in them defensively, for example through denial, avoidance, splitting, and acting out.

Abuse towards people with learning disabilities is far too common. Whilst counselling can not take away the experience of having been abused, listening, believing and giving the person a space to think about what has happened to them might just help to prevent them from being a victim again. Counselling may also help identify where abuse is expected or even elicited unconsciously, perhaps through the process of *repetition compulsion* where a person tries to gain control of what was overwhelming, or where abuse is repeated in the present by the victim becoming a perpetrator and going on to abuse others, perhaps through the process of *identification with the aggressor* as a way of dealing with their fear.

Bereavement and loss

It is a distressing fact that people with learning disabilities are likely to experience multiple concurrent losses. About 63 per cent of adults with learning disabilities live with their families in private households, the remaining 37 per cent live in communal residential care (Kavanagh and Opit, 1999). This means that with the death of one or both main parents or carers, people with learning disabilities have a great deal to lose in addition to the bereavement: their home, their neighbourhood, their possessions and their security. The term *transition shock* has been developed to describe the impact of multiple losses, and the responses to sudden changes that tend to accompany the loss (Coffman and Harris, 1980). Although people with learning disabilities are more likely to experience multiple losses throughout their lives, including the absent losses or 'what might have beens,' these experiences cannot really prepare for the terrible finality of a loss caused by death.

There have been several important studies exploring the experience of loss and bereavement for people with learning disabilities, and much of the work has focused on two main aspects, firstly, whether people with learning disabilities have a qualitatively or quantitatively different bereavement experience owing to their disabilities, and secondly, how staff manage client's loss.

Oswin (1981) undertook a large-scale study and concluded that people with learning disabilities are just as sensitive to the effects of a loss as others, and are just as likely to go through stages of grief. Brelstaff (1984) compared bereavement responses with IQs and found that bereavement reactions are not necessarily related to cognitive ability. It is now much clearer that people with learning disabilities are just as likely to go through a process of mourning that is characterised by stages, such as the model proposed by Parkes (1972). This means that their grief can take the form of anger, denial, yearning, distress and can take different forms at different points in time. The process of mourning is a working through of loss and anger with the person who has gone, so that eventually they feel forgiveness, allowing good feelings to be restored and new relationships to develop. The grief model also allows for mourning to be a long process, with anniversaries and significant dates often being particularly difficult or raising painful and distressing feelings. This may seem obvious, but it can be the case that it is painful to think about the reality of experience and therefore the expression of peoples' feelings can be denied, minimised, or even viewed as problematic.

In 1997 Hollins and Esterhuyzen published a study that explored the bereavement reactions in 50 parent-bereaved adults with learning disabilities using both interviews and checklists.

They found that frequently staff and carers did not attribute difficult behaviour to the bereavement, even though they were aware of the person's loss. There was no recognition of psychopathology being related to bereavement. Consequently there was a marked lack of appropriate counselling, and a minimisation of the importance of mementos and participation in rituals. Hollins and Esterhuyzen suggest that the impact of bereavement and its relationship to psychopathology is still underestimated.

Bicknell (1983) and Oswin (1991) have studied how people with learning disabilities' bereavements have been managed by carers and staff; their results indicate that there is a tendency to minimise or ignore the impact of loss. Oswin (1991) hypothesises four main reasons why this may be happening:

- staff may be afraid of their own responses, of becoming distressed or losing control of their own emotions when talking about death;
- they may be unsure how to comfort or control the emotions of the person with learning disabilities, and fear a response such as distress or anger;
- they may view the person with learning disabilities as not being able to understand the death, so it is not worth trying to explain; and
- they may also consider people with learning disabilities will not have the same emotional responses, so it will not matter if they are not informed.

Kloeppel and Hollins (1989) suggest that a family bereavement to a person with learning disabilities creates a double handicap, as both disability and death are taboo subjects. Both subjects elicit fearful avoidance. Like Oswin, they advocate allowing the space for people with learning disabilities to experience grief and to participate in the events surrounding the death, as well as, importantly, providing support and time to talk when needed.

Following these important studies, attitudes have started to shift and there is now wider recognition of the value for people with learning disabilities of the rituals associated with death such as saying good-bye, funerals and wakes. There are some helpful packs and guidelines designed for staff working with the learning disabled client group (Hollins and Sireling, 1991). Fortunately there is growing acknowledgement that people with learning disabilities do have 'normal' feelings and can experience the pain associated with loss that has often been denied of them. It is therefore important that there is an available relationship in which some of the thoughts and phantasies about death can be given words, thereby providing meaning to the turmoil, distress and confused feelings. Counselling can provide such a relationship.

CASE EXAMPLE: Mr Kapor

Mr Kapor is a man in his late forties who has a moderate learning disability. His keyworker, Ranjit, has become concerned about Mr Kapor because he has always been a gentle and warm-natured man, but recently has become more verbally aggressive in his responses to other people. He has also become more withdrawn and Ranjit suspects that Mr Kapor is depressed. He has tried to spend more time with Mr Kapor on his own, hoping this time would help him to talk more and to try and make more sense of his recent difficulties. Mr Kapor has lived in his current home for ten years now, before that he lived at home with his parents, up until his mother had died. His father did not feel able to look after Mr Kapor on his own so he was moved into residential care. His father visited him occasionally until nearly two years ago, at which point he had a stroke and could no longer visit. Mr Kapor was initially taken to the hospital to visit his father, but because his father had become so disabled by the stroke, staff decided that it would be too upsetting for Mr Kapor to visit. Mr Kapor did not seem to notice particularly, so when Mr Kapor's father died about a year ago the decision was made not to take Mr Kapor to the funeral. It was felt that it might stir him up too much, especially as he had become quite depressed following his mother's death, with whom he was reportedly very close.

Continued

Ranjit met with Mr Kapor in the office within the residential home. Mr Kapor sat and twisted his hair in an anxious way, and Ranjit sensitively commented that it seemed as if Mr Kapor was feeling quite worried. Mr Kapor started picking at his fingers and he said very quietly 'I haven't done anything, it wasn't me'. Ranjit said that Mr Kapor seemed to be thinking that Ranjit was cross with him or that it was hard for him to believe that he wasn't in trouble, but that this was a time for Mr Kapor to think about his worries. Mr Kapor looked at Ranjit and said 'you mean I'm not in trouble?' He then started to rock in his seat and Ranjit felt that Mr Kapor's anxiety level had significantly increased. He spoke out loud of his sense that Mr Kapor felt a great weight of responsibility and perhaps blame. Mr Kapor rocked silently in his chair for the rest of this meeting and Ranjit sat quietly with him, trying to understand what Mr Kapor might be feeling. At the end of the session, Ranjit offered Mr Kapor a further time to meet, and Mr Kapor looked relieved as he nodded in agreement.

At the next meeting, Mr Kapor again seemed to feel that he was 'in trouble', and was very anxious. Once more Ranjit talked about how he experienced Mr Kapor in the room, and this time Mr Kapor seemed to relax a little. As he relaxed, Ranjit talked about how Mr Kapor seemed to feel as if others were cross with him and Mr Kapor agreed, saying 'my dad too, he was always cross with me'. Ranjit was then able to explore Mr Kapor's feelings about his father's and mother's deaths, the guilt that he felt about his father's death particularly and his fears that he had contributed towards it. At some level it seemed that Mr Kapor was aware that it was the anniversary of his father's death and this seemed to be having a profound affect on him.

Ranjit is a very sensitive and thoughtful keyworker and his ability to stay with and try to make sense of Mr Kapor's negative feelings, rather than reassuring or ignoring them, seemed to help Mr Kapor think for himself. Mr Kapor's worries were perhaps made more conscious, enabling thinking about not only the actual relationships with his parents, but also the relationships that he had internalized and how he had experienced his internal relationships with them.

Mr Kapor's father's illness and subsequent death seemed to be the catalyst for his low mood and aggressive outbursts. Approaching the first anniversary seemed especially difficult for Mr Kapor, and the disturbed feelings it generated suggested that Mr Kapor may have had difficult and mixed feelings about his father. He seemed to be overwhelmed with phantasies that he would be reproached or punished for these feelings, and perhaps his fear that his angry phantasies had caused his father's death, and these conflicts seemed to be acted out in his current relationships. The loss of someone for whom we have mixed feelings can be especially difficult, as we may struggle with repressing more negative feelings, and these may then force themselves to the surface; this may have been the case with Mr Kapor.

Loss is a pervasive theme in counselling adults with learning disabilities, as the very nature of having a disability means there is a loss of what might have been. Being sensitive to a person's experience, allowing oneself to recognise loss as a real trauma is an important aspect of this work. Bereavement also needs proper consideration. Research suggests that people with learning disabilities' grief reactions are often underestimated, and not recognised as such. The space to talk or think together with someone about the feelings a bereavement can raise is a necessary and important aspect of work with this client group. However, one also needs to be mindful of the demands of this kind of work on the worker. Thinking about the loss of others can stir up feelings about one's own losses, and again supervision, training and personal therapy can help provide support and containment.

Challenging behaviour

Recent research has identified that between 5 and 15 per cent of people with learning disabilities regularly demonstrate behaviour defined as 'challenging' (Emerson et al., 2001). Behaviours that get subsumed within the label 'challenging' include aggression, destructive behaviour, self-injury, and any other behaviours that pose a risk to the health and safety of the person and people around them (Emerson et al., 2001).

There are defined risk factors associated with developing challenging behaviour which include: increasing severity of the learning disability, additional disabilities such as sensory impairment or communication difficulties, and certain diagnoses such as Autism or Lesch-Nyhan Syndrome (Emerson, 2001). Conceptualisation of challenging behaviour has shifted over the last few decades, from it being seen as a 'behavioural difficulty' within the person themselves, to the current view that it is behaviour that poses a *challenge to others*.

Within a counselling relationship, challenging behaviour can be helpfully viewed as a communication about a person's internal world. Behaviour can be employed to unconsciously recreate relationships, as was seen with Carley in Chapter 3, whose severe self-injurious behaviour served to communicate her sense of distress, or Denise in Chapter 2, whose aggressive and angry behaviour served to push people away, as she had come to expect would always happen. Having behaviour understood is essential for the mental health of the client. Workers may 'unintentionally' not understand the communication behind a behaviour to avoid confronting the pain often associated. Workers may need support, supervision and perhaps training to think about and understand processes and dynamics of behaviours. When behaviour is not understood, retaliation or increasingly difficult behaviour may result, or the client may just give up trying to get their message across and withdraw into a sense of helplessness.

In many respects the majority of the examples in this book represent behaviour that challenges others, and all behaviour needs to be thought about in the context of the person's life history and their immediate environment. For people with severely limited means of communication, the same behaviour may be used in many ways to represent many different emotional states, or states of mind. Sometimes it can be easier, and less painful, not to think about what the behaviour is communicating, but to just put it down to a personality trait – 'he always does that' – or to assign a permanent, consistent meaning to a behaviour – 'just ignore it when she says that, she only does it for attention'. The process of categorising behaviours negates the meaning for the person, and denies the possibility of any development in understanding, containing and thinking.

CASE EXAMPLE: Nicky

Nicky is a twenty-two-year-old man with a severe learning disability; he has epilepsy and is wheelchair-bound. He is hard of hearing and has very little language, although he can use a few Makaton signs and does occasionally use words to indicate his needs, though staff working with him feel he does this less and less. His keyworker, Lisa, at his day centre said it feels 'like he has just given up'. Nicky is incontinent of faeces and urine. He lives in residential care, a group home for three adults all with profound and multiple needs. He has lived there since he was eight years old, when his single mother said that she could no longer cope with him. She used to visit him every now and then, but after telling the home manager that she 'couldn't bear seeing him, as it made her feel too guilty and he did not notice her anyway' she stopped visiting him. He has not seen her since his fourteenth birthday.

At home and at his day centre Nicky has presented others with a difficulty in managing his behaviour. He is often unexpectedly aggressive and violent, hitting out at others or biting people very hard, without any warning. He smears his faeces frequently, normally when he is left on his own over himself and his chair, but he will also smear faeces on other people when he can.

Lisa, his keyworker, has been working with Nicky for about four years, since he started attending the centre. His special school also found Nicky challenging to manage, staff and other children tended to keep their distance from him, for fear of being hurt. Lisa has been hurt significantly by Nicky in the past, he bit her arm so hard that the bruise lasted three weeks, and she is aware of being careful of watching him for sudden movements when she is close to him. She is also aware that she finds his smearing disgusting and she feels angry with him when he does this. Nicky's difficult behaviours have been managed by reward systems that have tended to work for a few weeks, but then his difficult behaviour returns. Lisa would not have considered suggesting that Nicky have counselling as

Continued

he does not use much language and he does not seem to relate to anyone. However, she heard a talk about counselling with a person with severe learning difficulties who sounded similar to Nicky, so she contacted a mental health service she knew offered counselling to people with disabilities. She explained in the referral that she felt at a loss with Nicky, but wondered if he had the chance to talk whether he might use it. She knew that counselling did not always need language and she suspected that Nicky's behaviour, his smearing and aggression, must have some meaning.

Nicky was offered an assessment session at the clinic. Lisa brought him, and she asked if the counsellor would like her to come into the room with Nicky. The counsellor felt torn, she was aware that Nicky could be violent, but she wanted to offer him a respectful contact. She turned to Nicky and asked him what he wanted. Nicky gestured for Lisa to come with him. In the room, the counsellor talked about having a meeting together today, but next time perhaps Lisa could wait outside the room. Nicky looked more interested and gave an almost imperceptible nod. The counsellor listened as Lisa talked about Nicky, his background and difficulties, and Nicky too seemed to be aware; he sat quietly as she talked.

At the next meeting the counsellor found herself feeling very nervous, not about Nicky's behaviour, but about whether she would be able to understand his communications, or indeed whether she would be able to make herself understandable to Nicky. She wondered if he too felt nervous about this, about what they would make of each other. She sat watching Nicky and thinking about how he might be feeling, and she noticed that he too seemed to be studying her. She was able to talk about this, about how they were both trying to understand each other. Nicky looked intently at her. He then reached behind, into his trousers and produced a handful of faeces. He held it out to her as if to see what she would do. She felt repulsed, and thought to herself that she couldn't see him, she had underestimated how awful she could be made to feel and that he must want rid of her also. However, in thinking through these thoughts she felt calmer and less nauseous, and found her voice. She said, 'Nicky you are showing me just how shitty you feel, and perhaps you are wondering if I will be able to bear it'. He looked at her with curiosity and his hand lowered into his lap. The counsellor sat with him, thinking and watching and the mood in the room seemed less tense. At the end of the meeting, the counsellor said that they had another meeting together to decide if he would like to come and see her, but she had a regular time if he wanted it. At the next meeting Nicky was able to say yes to coming back. Work with Nicky was very slow, and often there would be periods of time where he would moan quietly to himself, or rock in his chair in a way that felt to the counsellor like she was being pushed out. Nicky continued to smear in the counselling sessions, especially when he became more distressed, but he only ever smeared himself or his wheelchair, never anything else in the room.

Working with challenging behaviour is demanding and it can be easier to walk away or distance oneself than to really confront any meaning that might be contained within challenging acts. Supervision, or a time for the counsellor to think with colleagues, can make the difference between a thoughtful approach and responding to the transference in a way that the person (unconsciously) expects and demands. It can also be difficult to explain to staff that the aim is not to remove the challenging behaviour itself, but to try and understand what the behaviour might be communicating at a conscious and a less conscious level. In Nicky's case, his difficult behaviour did slowly decrease, but with this he became increasingly depressed, as he came to understand some of his more painful feelings, particularly of rejection by his mother and his feelings about his disability; these two issues were very much linked in his mind (and indeed reality).

Mental health difficulties

The term 'mental health difficulties' can encompass a wide range of problems from neurotic difficulties such as anxiety and depression through to psychotic difficulties such as manic depression and schizophrenia. Often when a person has a psychiatric diagnosis as well as a learning disability then the term *dual diagnosis* is used. This term may not be very accurate because it is quite common for more than two diagnoses to be made, as learning disabilities frequently coexist with a range of other difficulties. These include mental health problems such as anxiety and depression, health difficulties such as epilepsy, sensory problems and genetic conditions such as Down's Syndrome, Fragile X Syndrome. The incidence of mental health difficulties in the general population is estimated at about 25 per cent (Goldberg and Huxley, 1980), but in with learning disabilities it is estimated that the incidence of serious mental health difficulties is up to 40 per cent (Iverson and Fox, 1989). Including the full range of milder emotional disorders pushes the estimates by some researchers to well over 50 percent of people with learning disabilities who experience mental health difficulties (Fraser and Nolan, 1995). This finding is perhaps not surprising given that people with learning disabilities are more likely to experience the risk factors associated with mental health difficulties such as loss, abuse and other aversive life events. They also have reduced access to potentially protective factors such as social support and financial security. The most common mental health difficulties in people with learning disabilities are affective disorders, particularly depression. However, psychotic disorders such as schizophrenia and manic depression are also over-represented within the learning disabilities population (Fraser and Nolan, 1995).

Mental health difficulties are notoriously difficult to reliably assess and diagnose in people with learning disabilities for several reasons (Emerson, 2001). These include:

- the overlap and interactions between mental health difficulties and challenging behaviour;
- the difficulty in assessing mental states in people with severe learning disabilities and communication difficulties;
- the use of diagnostic criteria that have not been standardised on the learning disabled population.

These difficulties, combined with the issue that mental health problems can have a significant negative impact on IQ, can make it very difficult to establish what aspects of a person's functioning are down to their learning difficulties and what aspects are due to their mental health difficulties.

Another significant problem for adults with a dual diagnosis is that of *'diagnostic overshadowing'* (Reiss, 1995). This is a process whereby symptoms or behaviours are either viewed as less important than the learning disability itself, or where the symptoms and behaviours are directly attributed to the learning disability rather than considering the presence of a psychiatric difficulty. For example, Clive is a thirty-two year old man with a moderate learning disability. He has a twin brother, Ian, who is of normal intelligence. Clive is particularly poor at self-care skills, and left to his own devices would not wash himself at all. He has also become erratic with his eating, sometimes binge eating and smearing food all over his clothes and at other times refusing food completely. This behaviour gave little cause for concern in his residential home; they put it down to his 'condition' of brain damage. However, when Ian started to look run-down and stopped looking after himself and when he started to behave oddly with his eating patterns, his wife quickly became concerned and asked him to see his doctor because she was worried that something might be wrong. Both men were later diagnosed with mental health difficulties, but Ian's diagnosis was made considerably earlier. In Clive's case, the diagnostic overshadowing of his learning disability got in the way of both recognising and understanding his behaviour.

People with learning disabilities who also have a mental illness can often find it difficult to access any kind of mental health services, as professionals may be divided about which service provider would be most appropriate: adult mental health or adult learning disabilities. Unfortunately this can mean that either an inappropriate service is provided or, worse still, no service is offered at all.

Assessing a person who has a dual diagnosis for counselling or therapy can be a complicated process. It is important that all the professionals and services involved in a person's care are in adequate communication, even before an individual assessment takes place. It is part of the assessment to establish how well the person's mental health difficulties are managed within their local community, and now with the recent legislation regarding the

Care Programme Approach and Clinical Governance (DoH, 1999) there is a requirement for risk assessment and care planning. External management of a person's situation is important, as they need a safe external environment before they can start to explore their internal world.

Counselling is a process that requires a person to be able to communicate and think together with another. It is therefore important that there is a capacity to facilitate this thinking process. Psychological and psychiatric disturbances that can interfere with thinking are likely to hinder the process of counselling. Therefore there are some mental health difficulties that may not be amenable to a counselling approach. For example, it is unwise to undertake an assessment of someone who is currently experiencing a psychotic episode, when their thinking is distorted or unrealistic. Any processes that hinder the capacity for self reflection will interfere with counselling and in these circumstances it would be more sensible to wait until both symptoms and thinking have stabilised. A psychiatrist will be able to help with the decision about when counselling might be viable. Another concern would be repeated psychotic episodes. When a person has had a number of 'breakdowns' over a relatively short period of time it could be hypothesised that having to think about their difficulties might be too much for them. A person needs to be robust enough or have sufficient ego strength to manage a more challenging approach. When the period of time between episodes is longer, such as several years, then it could well be possible to establish a helpful counselling relationship. Obviously it would be very important to work closely with the client's psychiatric team to ensure close monitoring and a containing wider system. Having all professional services such as health and social services linked up reduces the possibility of splitting and mixed messages.

Having a diagnosis of a serious mental health difficulty such as schizophrenia or manic depression need not exclude a person from being offered some form of counselling. When the nature of their difficulties has been well established and they are on medication to control or relieve their symptoms, or they are in remission from symptoms for a substantial period of time, an individual assessment will establish the viability of counselling.

CASE EXAMPLE: Ms Moncrieffe

Ms Moncrieffe is a forty-five year old woman with a dual diagnosis of mild learning disability and schizophrenia. She has been kept fairly stable on antipsychotic medication that also has a tranquillising effect. She has not had a psychotic breakdown for three years now, and she has never attempted suicide or presented with aggressive or threatening behaviour. She also suffers from epilepsy for which she takes regular medication. She lives in sheltered accommodation with six other residents all of whom have psychiatric diagnoses as well as learning disabilities.

Ms Moncrieffe had her first psychotic breakdown when she was eighteen. At the time she was living at home with her adoptive parents. After leaving school she became more withdrawn and uncommunicative. Eventually she became quite confused and was found wandering around late at night, unable to say what she was doing. Her behaviour became erratic with swings from being withdrawn and quiet to loud and incoherent. She became more paranoid, worrying that people were talking about her, and it was eventually established that on occasions she experienced hallucinatory voices, saying that she was 'stupid and no good'. She was admitted to a psychiatric hospital following an episode when she locked herself in her room for several days and refused to eat as she believed her adoptive mother was trying to poison her. She recovered relatively quickly from this psychotic episode, however she has had further breakdowns at intervals of roughly four to six years since then.

She currently attends a day centre for people with learning disabilities, and her keyworker at the centre felt she might benefit from the opportunity to talk to someone removed from her immediate environment, hence a referral for counselling. Ms Moncrieffe has had a few temporary jobs which she has managed successfully, including stacking shelves in a supermarket and cleaning. Over the last six years she has not been working, which she has put down to her illness; it is apparent that she has been of low mood for some time now.

Continued

Ms Moncrieffe had been attending once-weekly counselling for about eighteen months before her mental health started to deteriorate. She had made a good link with her counsellor, and although she clearly found it painful, she was able to talk about what worried her. She had been very preoccupied with her family of origin. She knew that her birth mother was also a diagnosed schizophrenic and that she was her mother's sixth child. She knew nothing about her father, but it was clear that her parents' relationship had been brief. She also knew that of the five other children, only two had remained with her mother. Ms Moncrieffe became overwhelmed with her feelings of rejection, that her mother had kept some children but not her. The experience of sorrow, anger and rage in the room with Ms Moncrieffe at times felt overwhelming for her counsellor. Ms Moncrieffe was filled with phantasies that she was unwanted because of her disabilities, and that there was something dreadfully wrong 'with her insides'. She revealed that when she was twenty-three she had become pregnant, through a casual relationship, but that she had miscarried the baby quite late in the pregnancy. Her fears and fantasies about her baby were painful to experience, her thoughts about whether the child too would have been 'stupid and mad', and how she had destroyed the baby by the way in which she had projected her own feelings of 'stupidity and madness' into it.

Eighteen months into her treatment, the keyworker that had originally referred her told Ms Moncrieffe that she was pregnant, and that she would be going on maternity leave in three months' time.

Ms Moncrieffe became much more withdrawn in her therapy sessions, and her ability to make links between her feelings and behaviours diminished. She became gradually more paranoid, and started to miss sessions, telling staff in her residential home that her counsellor did not like her, and had said that she was 'fat and smelly'. In counselling sessions she became more aggressive, pointing her finger in jabbing movements at the counsellor saying 'I know you are talking about me, I know that you know my mother and you have been talking together about how to get rid of me'. The counsellor tried to make links for Ms Moncrieffe between her distrustful, anxious feelings and the impending loss of her keyworker, but Ms Moncrieffe seemed to have lost the capacity to think. She stopped coming to her sessions completely. It seemed as if her feelings of persecution had taken her over, leaving her out of touch with reality. The counsellor discussed Ms Moncrieffe's withdrawal and odd behaviour with Ms Moncrieffe's psychiatrist, who also had concerns. A network meeting was convened, attended by Ms Moncrieffes's GP, the psychiatrist, the counsellor and representatives from her home and daycare. It was decided that it would be necessary to monitor Ms Moncrieffe very closely and that she would need to be admitted into hospital for this. The counsellor wrote to Ms Moncrieffe in hospital saying that she could return to her counselling as soon as she felt well enough.

Ms Moncrieffe remained in hospital for four months. She was discharged with the support of a CPN. Three months after her discharge she was able, of her own volition, to return to the counselling.

Ms Moncrieffe's case highlights the need for good communication between agencies and professionals, especially when there are anxieties about mental health. The work with Ms Moncrieffe also illustrates how having a diagnosis of a psychotic condition is not necessarily a complete bar to being able to use a psychotherapeutic approach, but work may need to include breaks at times when a person is not able to manage the intensive nature of counselling. In Ms Moncrieffe's case she had a solid network of support in the community to hold her until she felt able to continue her counselling.

Sensory impairments

Sensory impairments are highly correlated with learning disabilities. A large-scale study published in 1989 found that 48 per cent of people with learning disabilities have one sensory impairment of at least moderate severity, and 18 per cent had more than one sensory impairment (Office of Population Censuses and Surveys,

1989). Another study estimated that among people with learning disabilities, one in three people has a sensory impairment (Harries, 1991). Many of these people could have their impairments corrected, but unfortunately the identification of difficulties is poorly managed. For example, in a Mencap study of adults of whom over two-thirds were over forty (the age from which sight commonly deteriorates), 53 per cent had not had a sight test in the previous two years (Kerr, 1998). It is also commonly the case that people with Down's syndrome experience gradual hearing loss as they get older.

Sensory impairments can interfere with the development of relationships at an early profound level. If we think about the importance of the developing relationship between an infant and his or her main carer, the need to be able to hear tones of voice, or to see the warmth and understanding reflected in onlooking eyes becomes all the more important. If there are problems accessing normal containing, nurturing experiences due to visual, auditory or other sensory difficulties, then problematic relationships may be internalised and continue to have an ongoing impact on subsequent relationships, through the life of a person's internal world or object relations. Visual and other sensory problems fall high on lists of stressful aspects of caring for children with disabilities (Seligman and Darling, 1989; Dale, 1995).

Sensory difficulties may interfere with development and relationships throughout the life span. It is more difficult to establish relationships with others when you cannot use the mediums of speech and vision. Adaptations for people of normal intelligence may not be as accessible to people with learning disabilities because they are more likely to have physical disabilities and so cannot use adaptations such as Braille, or may not have the cognitive skills to access different mediums of communication such as sign systems. It is not difficult to see how someone who cannot hear or see might retreat into their own world, giving up the struggle to make others understand. When working with adults with sensory difficulties it is important to understand and be aware of how they communicate. This may mean working with those who are close to the client, to learn how to approach them. For example, it is important to know how to let them know where you are, when they might have to move, how they express likes and dislikes. Working with adults with learning disabilities and especially those with physical and sensory problems often requires much greater flexibility of approach than working with other client groups. It may, for example, be necessary to make physical contact to help them move or even to help them indicate their needs. Communication may need to take place through gestures or movement, vocalisations – not necessarily words – and even through songs and singing. Working with the client, at the level they present with, whilst maintaining respectful contact can be a real challenge.

CASE EXAMPLE: Nisha

Nisha is a twenty-two-year-old woman with a severe learning disability. She is almost completely blind and has a hearing impairment. She also has physical disabilities, is wheelchair-bound and has little independent movement. She lives at home with her parents and her seventeen-year-old sister, Sarita. Nisha's mother, Mrs Gupta, asked her GP if she could talk to a counsellor about her daughter, from whom she has been feeling increasingly distant. The referral from the GP stated that Nisha and her mother have always been very close. Mrs Gupta has been Nisha's main carer, and they have developed a way of understanding each other, through touch and movements as well as the small amount of vocalisations that Nisha makes.

The whole family was invited together for the first appointment, but only Mrs Gupta and Nisha attended this meeting with the counsellor. Nisha appeared to be a very disabled and young looking woman in a wheelchair. She had long dark hair that was very beautifully plaited and decorated. Mrs Gupta was a small, tired and worn-looking woman. Mrs Gupta sat on a chair very close to Nisha, holding her hand tightly. Mrs Gupta started by saying that she and Nisha have a very special relationship as Nisha cannot communicate with other people in the way that she can with her. Nisha seemed to turn her head slightly away from her mother as she spoke, and when the counsellor asked about this, Mrs Gupta said that Nisha could

Continued

not hear very much at all. Mrs Gupta went on to say that she was worried about Nisha who seemed to be more withdrawn and unhappy recently. The meeting was spent thinking together about Nisha's history. Mrs Gupta dominated the meeting, saying that Nisha wouldn't be able to understand, hear or see anything so was very dependent on her, so there was 'no point' in a counsellor meeting with Nisha on her own. She then talked in a matter of fact way about all the 'necessary' sacrifices she had made for Nisha, such as giving up work to look after her, and only having one more child when she would have liked more. After the meeting the counsellor was filled with an overwhelming feeling of frustration. She thought about Nisha's feelings, that perhaps Nisha's experience was of frustration; she thought about Nisha's presentation, like a little girl, although she was actually twenty-one, and she thought of her difficulties in communicating and interacting. The counsellor then thought about Mrs Gupta, how some of the frustration might be hers: her sacrifices and Nisha's dependency on her. In the next meeting the counsellor was able to raise some of these thoughts with Mrs Gupta and Nisha. Mrs Gupta responded by releasing Nisha's hand and Nisha moaned loudly and insistently. Mrs Gupta said that she had thought about Nisha having time with a counsellor, and that she would be able to explain a Braille-like symbol system they had developed in conjunction with the local speech and language therapy service. She acknowledged that although Nisha had very little speech, she did have some residual hearing. She said 'sometimes it's easier not to think that Nisha might actually be able to hear other people'. Following this assessment, both Nisha and her mother were offered individual sessions with counsellors, and both of them were able to take up this offer.

Nisha and her mother's experiences to some degree demonstrate some of the difficulties that can develop very early on when a child has complex sensory, physical and learning difficulties. Over time during the therapy Mrs Gupta was able to think about her relationship with her daughter, her initial feelings of anger and overprotectiveness that seemed to have contributed to the very close and now stifling relationship that had grown up between them. In the individual sessions with Nisha, her abilities to hear more than had previously thought became more apparent. However, Nisha was quite resistant to meeting with her counsellor, indicating very clearly that she did not want to talk. One might hypothesise that Nisha found it too painful to be in touch with the realities of her life as a twenty-one-year old with all her limitations and losses. However, only by becoming in touch and developing the ability to tolerate her limitations will she be able to make contact with her strengths and competencies. Withdrawing from thinking also cuts her ability to recognise these.

SUMMARY

- In this chapter some of the most common 'reasons for referral' have been considered, such as abuse, challenging behaviour and bereavement.
- Mental health difficulties have also been considered. People with learning disabilities are more prone to developing mental health difficulties, and to having negative life experiences such as losses and abuse. This occurs for a number of reasons, such as increased vulnerability due to poor resources and language, having numerous professionals involved and greater physical vulnerabilities.
- Working with people with learning disabilities can be extremely distressing, especially if one allows oneself to experience all their projections and recognise their realities. Support for this is needed on several levels including proper supervision, training and personal therapy.

6

RELATIONSHIP ISSUES: FAMILIES AND INTIMATE RELATIONSHIPS

Nancy Sheppard

Relationships with other people have an important role in shaping our personalities, our experiences and how we feel about ourselves. In the past, relatively little attention was paid to the relationships of people with learning disabilities.

This chapter will aim to address some of the additional difficulties that people with learning disabilities may experience in their relationships. It should be noted that it is not inevitable that people with learning disabilities have relationship difficulties, but when an individual is seeking help for any difficulties they are experiencing it is important to consider their relationships with others. I will initially consider relationships with family members, then focus on intimate relationships and people with learning disabilities as parents. Individuals' experiences of relationships breaking down will be also be considered.

Early family relationships

A child's relationship with their parents begins as early as the moment when the pregnancy is discovered. It has long been established that there is a link between mental health problems in children and the attitudes and behaviours of their parents towards them. Maternal depression, the parents' own childhood experiences and their experiences of being parented can all influence parental states of mind and attitudes towards a parenting role; in Chapter 2 Bion's concept of containing and container between infant and object (parent) was described. Ricky Emmanuel (1984) uses the term 'primary disappointment' to describe the child's experience when his or her innate expectation of discomfort being contained by an object (parent) is not realised. Louise Emmanuel (1997) extends this concept to include a disappointment in the mother when she realises that she has a limited capacity for containment of a child with a disability. She postulates that the mother may never recover from this 'primary disappointment' and as a result, where thinking and understanding usually develop and allow the infant's intelligence to flourish, both the child's and the parent's experiences becomes locked in reciprocal projections of disappointment and loss.

Inevitably new parents compare their children to their peers and although all children develop at different rates, a disability can intensify the feelings associated with unfavourable comparisons. Confirmation of these differences through diagnosis of a learning disability can be devastating. Other parents may find themselves very alone in the first months with a nagging feeling that all is not well but receive little support for their suspicions and feel they are fighting to be heard. Parents in this group may report a sense of relief in being given a diagnosis, at last being believed or vindicated when a difficulty is identified.

Once a diagnosis has been made or a disability identified, many parents experience an enormous and complex system of professionals becoming involved in their child's care, each person giving advice and support. Decisions can be painful and difficult when the parents are still reeling from the news that their child is not the 'perfect child' that they had been expecting for nine months. Diagnosis can lead to parents going over and over their experiences searching for reasons why things have gone wrong. Blaming themselves and one another can lead to rifts in relationships at a time when togetherness and mutual support is most important.

CASE EXAMPLE: Sinead

Sinead is a mother of five children. She was referred soon after the birth of her fifth child. Her second child, Rhiannon, was diagnosed with Cerebral Palsy at birth and her youngest child, Connor, had been diagnosed with a rare genetic condition, associated with severe learning disabilities and dysmorphic features. During the counselling sessions Sinead described her acute feelings of despair and shame when she saw people looking into her pram and seeing her children looking so 'different'. She said that she was left feeling an overwhelming sense of guilt that she could be ashamed of her children. In exploring these feelings further, Sinead said that she had not felt these difficult feelings so deeply and intensely when caring for just one disabled child. She felt that she had been able to develop a very special relationship with her daughter Rhiannon, now eight years old. She felt she was able to see through Rhiannon's disabilities to the 'bright and bubbly little girl'.

Sinead was very clear, however, that she felt she had not been able to bond well with Connor. She talked about her hopes during her pregnancy but also an underlying fear that all would not be well. She described feeling overwhelmed by joy when Connor was born. However, within days she sensed that something was wrong and did not feel close to Connor. She struggled to nurse him and found it difficult to be with him. Her GP and health visitor were concerned that she might be developing postnatal depression. Sinead remained convinced that something was wrong. Connor was four months old before any investigations took place and his genetic condition was eventually diagnosed. Sinead described feeling furious that no one had believed her, relieved that she was not going mad and totally devastated about Connor's prognosis. Sinead found all of these feelings overwhelming and felt she could not cope. She and her husband had decided to have Connor fostered and she requested counselling to try to help her address her feelings about Connor and the fostering.

Sinead used her sessions to think about her expectations of

parenting. She drew on her experience of her relationship with her mother, who she felt could cope with anything. She felt she had failed her children but that she would be failing them further if she kept Connor, as she would not be available to the other children, particularly as Rhiannon needed so much additional support.

Sinead believed that the professionals supporting her and her family thought she should keep Connor. She experienced the social workers as judgemental, blaming and obstructive. Through her counselling sessions we were able to explore these experiences and Sinead developed some insight into how her internal world was impacting on her experience of other people. She was able to understand that some of the persecutory feelings she was experiencing from the professionals she was in contact with were a projection of her feelings about herself; she was judging herself harshly. Sinead remained convinced that the best solution for her and her family was for Connor to be cared for outside the family. During the period of counselling Connor was fostered. Sinead was clear that she could not allow herself to bond with Connor in order for this to occur. She found his disabilities unbearable. This was clearly a very sensitive and difficult situation to manage as a counsellor. Sinead was also able to use the counselling sessions to explore her feelings about Rhiannon. I felt that it was possible that Sinead was strongly projecting all of the difficult feelings she had about Rhiannon's birth and her disabilities into Connor to enable her to mother Rhiannon. It was important to help Sinead to bring this defensive position into her conscious thought in order that she could make a clear decision about Connor's future.

Later experiences

Goldberg *et al.* (1995) use systems theory to explore families' responses to having a disabled family member. They suggest that families may re-experience feelings of loss, anger and blame associated with the birth of a disabled child at subsequent life-cycle stages. Emmanuel (1997) proposes that parents may re-experience the 'primary disappointment' of learning of their child's disabilities and difference at each transition and milestone.

CASE EXAMPLE: Jean

In her individual therapy Jean talked about the pressure she felt from her parents to behave 'like a grown-up' and to 'act her age', yet reported not being allowed to go out alone or to have relationships with people she wanted to. Jean felt she was expected to overcome her difficulties despite having been diagnosed with a moderate learning disability in early childhood. In work with her parents the counsellor helped to explore the feelings that lay behind Jean's complaints. It became clear they were clinging to the hope that Jean might grow up and 'overcome' her difficulties thereby 'saving' her family from having to grieve the permanence of her disabilities. As well as being frequently reminded of her parents' disappointment, Jean also faced her own sense of disappointment and despair that her hopes – wishing to have a relationship and possibly her own family, to move away from her parents' home and to have a job – were not being fulfilled.

Goldberg *et al.* (1995) propose that dilemmas similar to those of Jean's family are linked to the family's need to protect the person with learning disabilities from the perceived consequences of their disability. During her counselling sessions this issue of protection was explored. Jean described getting into situations in which she could be vulnerable. For instance, she had been attending a group at a local college near her home. It was routine for her father to meet her at the gate after the end of the session. On one occasion Jean said she had finished the group early and someone outside the college had offered her a lift. She said that she knew she should not go with strangers and had walked home. Over the next few days she engaged in conversation with the man outside the college. When her dad came to pick her up he was shocked to see her talking to someone they did not know, and got into an argument with the man. Jean talked about this incident with concern but it became clear that she had wanted her dad to see her. The counsellor wondered about her motivation in relation to this incident as it had occurred around the time that her mum was due to go into hospital for a major operation. The counsellor wondered if Jean's risky behaviour might be distracting from the frightening reality of her mother's ill health. If Jean started to act in a responsible and adult manner, her parents would no longer need to worry about her and might have to face, not only their own mortality but also their painful repressed emotions around Jean's disability.

This type of interdependency is often seen in families with a learning disabled member. Sinason (1992) suggests that the issue of dependency needs to be addressed in order for a person with learning disabilities to be freed up in their thinking. Once Jean was able to acknowledge her worries about her mother's ill health and the true nature of her emotional and physical dependency on her parents she found that she was able to negotiate with her father and to be able to attend her sessions without her parents escorting her.

In Jean's family, members acted in ways that protected each other from real and perceived dangers. This can be seen as a strength and coping strategy in the face of considerable adversity. However, as Goldberg *et al.* (1995) noted, when a family is engaged in such intense efforts to protect each other from the painful effects of grief, this can often impose great costs on the lives of individual family members. Requests for help with behaviour difficulties from parents are common, yet it is not unusual to find that following initial success of interventions change can be difficult to maintain and old behaviours soon return. Bower (1995) suggests that the blocks a counsellor may experience in offering parents advice result from repressed painful memories of their own childhood experiences of being parented. These painful memories might include the initial difficult feelings experienced at the birth of a disabled child. Although parents may be motivated to change the situation, unless the counsellor addresses the emotional impact of early feelings the situation is likely to remain stuck.

CASE EXAMPLE: Jonathon

Jonathon is an eighteen-year-old man with moderate learning disabilities who attends a special school. At the parents' request, initial consultations over three months focused on his difficult behaviour at home and at school. The parents dutifully took away the therapist's advice and on each occasion would return the next month with reports of some successes. However, as soon as they made any progress with one of Jonathon's difficult behaviours, another, more challenging, behaviour developed. The counsellor felt that the difficulties might lie in the painful feelings that the parents had experienced in accepting Jonathon's difficulties. At this point, it became clear that Jonathon's behaviour was becoming too difficult for them to manage at home and they considered the option of residential college. Jonathon's social worker arranged for several weeks of respite care during this crisis until an appropriate college was found. During this period the parents found it increasingly difficult to think about Jonathon going away. It became apparent that for many years Jonathon's behaviour had masked some serious difficulties in their own relationship and had prevented them from addressing these issues. With Jonathon in a temporary respite placement his parents found themselves faced with the reality that there was a strong possibility that their own relationship would break down. They agreed to change the focus of the sessions to think about some aspects of their relationship and the impact of having a child with learning disabilities. Over the next few months they were able to talk about the disappointment and subsequent guilt that they had experienced on learning of Jonathon's disabilities. Both parents were able to acknowledge that they blamed one another for Jonathon being disabled, and were angry with one another about the circumstances around his birth. With the social worker's assistance the family found a local college for Jonathon and a regular respite facility. The parents continued to work with the counsellor and reported that the situation gradually became more tolerable, with Jonathon responding better to the boundaries that his parents set and the parents more able to communicate clearly with one another about their grievances.

Carter and McGoldrick's (1980) 'family life-cycle' theory describes the typical sequence of life-cycle transitions that families
negotiate, such as the birth of a child, starting school, leaving
home and setting up home of their own. Their theory considers
how stressors, such as family patterns, myths and secrets, can
facilitate or hinder the process of transition. Vetere (1993) notes
that in families where one member has a disability, the sequence
of life events is often different. Often life-cycle transitions in such
families can appear out of synchrony with same age peers, as is
illustrated in work with Tom.

CASE EXAMPLE: Tom

Tom is forty-nine years old, lives at home and attends a day
centre for people with learning disabilities. His parents are
elderly and over the past two years Tom's mother has become
increasingly confused with memory problems and the GP was
concerned that she was developing the first signs of dementia.
The family were referred because Tom had started to be verbally aggressive at the day centre. Tom has an older sister who
has her own family and lives nearby. It was recently established that his sister would not be in a position to care for Tom
when his parents eventually die. Unlike the majority of forty-
nine-year-old men, Tom never spent any significant time away
from his parents, yet with his mother's deteriorating condition
the family had just begun to consider the possibility of respite
care. The couple used sessions to think about the future and
the changes they could have to face. Tom's father felt that if it
weren't for his wife's increasing difficulties meeting Tom's
needs, they would not need to think about these issues.

Todd and Shearn (1996) explored different parenting styles in a
group of parents of adults with learning disabilities. One of the
parenting styles identified was observed in parents they named
'perpetual parents'. 'Perpetual parents' conveyed a sense that
their predominant identity was as parents of the child with a
learning disability, their social contacts were primarily with other

parents of adults with learning disabilities and they tended to cast doubt on anyone else's capacity to care for their child. Both Tom and Jean's parents could be described as taking up the role of 'perpetual parents'. They had few opportunities for time alone as a married couple or to pursue other roles and interests away from constant supervision of their son or daughter. Grant (1986) found that carers were reluctant to pass on what they saw as their caring responsibility to others, possibly because the role enabled them to feel competent and self-sufficient. Tom's parents described with pride how they had coped alone and expressed the fear that receiving help from others might be perceived as a sign that they could no longer cope. An important function of the 'perpetual parents' role may be its power as a defence against the pain of the reality of a person's disabilities

Sibling relationships

Relationships with siblings are likely to be the longest lasting and perhaps the most complex relationships for people with learning disabilities. An estimated 80 per cent of children with disabilities have non-disabled siblings (Atkinson and Crawford, 1995). Sibling relationships exist within a context of family relationships, parenting style, birth order and individual characteristics. All these factors influence the relationships between siblings and add to their complexity. Psychodynamic theorists have been particularly interested in sibling relationships and it is well established that sibling rivalry, negativity and jealousy between siblings is a normal part of growing up with brothers and sisters. Sibling rivalry is largely considered as an important factor in the development of personalities (Dunn and Kendrick, 1982). The birth of a sibling can raise jealous feelings, but when in reality a sibling is born damaged in some way, the omnipotent phantasies can be experienced as having a life of their own. Whenever phantasies become reality it can lead to emotional difficulties both within the sibling relationships and in the family as a whole.

Much of the research in this area has been from non-disabled siblings' perspectives and the literature suggests learning disabilities can have both benefits and disadvantages for siblings, and both positive and negative effects on relationships between

siblings. In a review of the literature focusing on literature exploring relationships of siblings of people with learning disabilities,
Boyce and Barnett (1993) cite disagreement among both early
and more recent studies. For example, when Gath (1974) compared groups of siblings of learning disabled children, siblings of
non-disabled children and children with minor disabilities (such
as cleft palate) she found higher levels of behaviour problems
in the siblings of children with learning disabilities. Powell and
Gallagher (1993) surveyed attitudes towards having a sibling with
learning disabilities and found high levels of role-tension (defined
as frustration, tension and anxiety). Burke and Montgomery
(2000) suggest that children with a sibling with a learning disability receive less attention from their parents because of the additional care given to the person with learning disability needs.

In terms of positive effects, Gath and Gumley (1987) found
no significant differences in behaviour between groups with or
without learning disabled siblings. Carr (1988) undertook a
longitudinal study to measure reported behaviour problems in a
group of siblings of children with Down's syndrome against those
of a matched comparison group. She found none of the mothers
of children with Down's Syndrome reported significant behaviour difficulties in siblings, whilst three families in the comparison group did. Carr concluded that mothers of children with
Down's syndrome judged other children in the family to be
relatively well adjusted.

Miller (1974) explored relationships between siblings with and
without learning disabilities by asking them about the kinds of
activities they did together. The results suggested a tendency for
participants to describe activities with learning-disabled siblings
in terms of care giving or helping activities, whilst they reported
play activities with non-disabled siblings. Miller also found that
respondents reported more positive affect towards learning-
disabled siblings than non-disabled siblings suggesting that
relationships with siblings with learning disabilities are different
from other sibling relationships.

Burke and Montgomery (2000) reported both positive and
negative comments from children with a sibling with learning-
disabilities and note the additional care-giving responsibilities
that these children tend to take on. They stress the importance of
sibling support groups in helping children with learning-disabled

siblings to explore their experiences, to help reduce their anxieties and concerns, and to adjust to the difference that they might perceive in their lives. Evans *et al.* (2001) agree; a sibling support group they evaluated proved to be helpful in terms of improving involvement between siblings, improving self-esteem and increasing knowledge of learning disabilities associated with challenging behaviour.

Studies of relationships between adult siblings suggest that most adult siblings are involved in the lives of their sibling with a learning disability and that the relationships were generally viewed as positive (Seltzer *et al.*, 1991) This study also demonstrated that the quality of relationships was hierarchical, for instance, non-disabled siblings provided help and support to their sibling with a disability. There was some evidence of learning-disabled siblings attempting to offer reciprocal, helping relationships such as offers of babysitting for non-disabled families.

There is very little literature that looks at people with learning disabilities' views of their relationships with their siblings. This may be, in part, attributed to methodological difficulties in research with people with learning disabilities but it might also relate to the acutely painful feelings that people with learning disabilities may experience in comparing themselves to their able siblings.

CASE EXAMPLE: Lehman

The Lee family were referred for family counselling by their GP, as they had not been getting on well together. The family consists of three brothers, Chin, Lehman (who has learning disabilities) and Ming.

Lehman lived with his younger brother Ming and Ming's wife. During an assessment interview with the Lee family, Ming and his older brother Chin talked about their experience of growing up with Lehman. The brothers gave two very different accounts of their relationship with Lehman. Ming remembered feeling frightened by Lehman's epileptic seizures and worrying about him at school when he had one of his frequent admissions to hospital following a particularly bad seizure.

Chin, on the other hand, explained that he was four years old when Lehman was born. He said that his most salient memory of his childhood following Lehman's birth was a feeling of resentment towards his younger brother as his mother always seemed to be too tired to spend time playing with him because of tending to Lehman's needs or taking Lehman to hospital. Over the period of the assessment both brothers talked more openly about their feelings about having a brother with learning disabilities. In one particularly difficult session Chin revealed that, underneath his feelings of resentment, lay a deep sense of guilt. He nervously told his brother and the counsellor that he had always felt he was responsible for Lehman's epilepsy. He described a situation where he had felt really angry because his mother had said she was too tired to read him a bedtime story. He had screamed and cried in his tantrum and kicked his mother's pregnant stomach. She had put him down immediately and shouted at him; he said he remembered clearly that when she was shouting she was rubbing her stomach. Lehman was born six weeks prematurely and consequently spent several weeks in a special baby care unit. Chin said that he had always worried that it was his kick that caused the damage.

Intimate relationships

The social barriers for people with learning disabilities to develop intimate or sexual relationships are complex. In addition to the obstacles people with learning disabilities experience in meeting others and making friends, there are additional problems to face in terms of attitudes to their sexuality, vulnerability to abusive or exploitative sexual relationships and barriers to consent.

With the development of 'Normalisation' (Wolfensberger, 1972) and the subsequent publication in the UK of 'Better Services for People with Mental Handicaps' (1971) a number of authors turned their attention to the sexual rights of people with learning disabilities and thus allowed a forum for thinking more liberally about sexuality and people with learning disabilities. Craft (1987) proposed six human rights relating to sexuality for people with learning disabilities that she felt had, in many cases, previously been violated:

- The right to grow up – to be treated with the respect and dignity accorded to adults.
- The right to know – to have access to as much information about themselves and their bodies and those of other people, their emotions, appropriate social behaviour, and so forth, as they can assimilate.
- The right to be sexual and make and break relationships.
- The right not to be at the mercy of the individual sexual attitudes of different caregivers.
- The right not to be sexually abused.
- The right to humane and dignified environments.

From Craft's groundbreaking work in the field of learning disabilities and sexuality a number of related debates have arisen. Once the right to intimate relationships and a sexual life began to be accepted, the issue of capacity to consent to such a relationship and making informed decisions about one's relationships became paramount. People with learning disabilities have historically had little power to make decisions, including decisions about relationships. The 1997 White Paper 'Who Decides?' aims to ensure government policy supports people to make decisions for themselves wherever possible. The issue of decision making and establishing consent is extremely complex and needs to be evaluated case by case. As a result numerous debates have been proposed in both the academic and policy-making literature; to do this issue justice is beyond the scope of this chapter. A detailed account of consent issues for people with learning disabilities can be found in Craft (1994).

Several writers have considered the issue of sexuality of people with learning disabilities (Craft and Brown, 1994, McCarthy 2001, and Burns 2000). Literature concerning gay and lesbian relationships of people with learning disabilities is scarce and often fails to associate sexual orientation with being a gay person and the positive cultural aspects that are associated with a 'gay identity'. More often relationships are described purely in terms of the sexual acts, for instance, as a man having sex with another man or woman choosing a same sex partner (Cambridge, 1997b).

In addition to the practical barriers for people with learning disabilities in developing intimate, sexual relationships there are also psychological taboos around the issue of sexuality. Sinason (1992) wrote of her experiences in therapy with people with learning disabilities and concluded that thinking about procreation, how they came to be born, and consequently their beliefs and fantasies about their own sexuality, was an important task for therapy in order to help an individual address the pain of their disability and difference. She observed that many of her patients had a fantasy of bad sex having created them as a disabled person. Their own sexual development became arrested and they were left with disturbed or disrupted beliefs and ideas about sexual relationships. This can become a barrier to forming healthy sexual relationships and leaves the individual vulnerable to exploitation and abuse. As people with learning disabilities are vulnerable to experiencing abusive relationships it is not surprising that it is less common to encounter referrals for couple therapy or sexual problems. However, Sheppard (1991) published an account of sex therapy for both individuals and couples with learning difficulties, in which she described helping with disabilities of a sexual nature.

The following case example gives an illustration how individuals' feelings about disability and sexuality can manifest as difficulties in intimate relationships.

CASE EXAMPLE: Mr Hall and Ms Brown

Mr Hall and Ms Brown were referred to the team following some concerns about their relationship. Mr Hall was described as having a borderline learning disability and Ms Brown a mild learning disability and some physical disabilities (scoliosis). They lived together in a supported living project. A team of support workers came in on a daily basis for three to four hours to support the couple and help with everyday activities including Ms Brown's personal care, budgeting, household chores and outings. Mr Hall found he was becoming increasingly possessive of his partner. He described feeling angry when

Continued

Ms Brown spoke to shopkeepers or talked about people whom she knew on her college course. He said that he didn't like Ms Brown laughing with the support workers when they were helping her. Ms Brown complained that Mr Hall was acting 'mean and horrible' and on one occasion had 'completely lost it'. The counsellor wondered if anyone else was around at this time. Ms Brown said that Fiona (her support worker) had just left after having helped her with her bath.

During the counselling session it became clear that although he valued his relationship with Ms Brown very highly, Mr Hall found any intrusion on this relationship intolerable. He said that he felt jealous and didn't like the fact that he could not help Ms Brown with everything she needed help with. He was worried about the strength of his feelings and how angry he could feel. He said he was scared that Ms Brown would leave him. The couple then talked about previous relationships. Mr Hall mentioned his relationship with his parents. He had found his father frightening and had witnessed extreme violence from his father towards his mother. He said he could not do anything to stop his father and felt bad about that. He could not understand how his mum had 'stood for it', but when his dad was in a good mood they were loving together. Over a number of sessions it became clear that Mr Hall was able to make a link between his frightened and angry feelings about his parents' relationship and the feelings he had when Ms Brown was chatty to other people, particularly men. The issue with the support workers was complicated; the counsellor felt that both Ms Brown and Mr Hall were projecting their difficult feelings about their disabilities into one another and into the support workers.

In addition to the relationship difficulties they were experiencing, the referral letter noted that staff were unsure if Mr Hall and Ms Brown were having a sexual relationship. They shared a bedroom and a bed. It was six months into therapy before either of them mentioned having difficulties in their sexual relationship. In this session the couple began, as usual, with a long and complicated story of who had said what to whom and why they had ended up having an argument. This was followed by what felt like a long and painful silence, with Mr Hall fidgeting nervously in his chair and staring at Ms Brown as if willing her to speak. The counsellor wondered if she might be thinking about something that Mr Hall had said that she found difficult, she looked down and nodded. Mr Hall asked her what was the matter but she said she couldn't say. The long silences continued but with the help of careful and sensitive interpretations, over the next few sessions Ms Brown was able to articulate that the issue she found so painful to talk about was her fear of becoming pregnant and that between them they would inevitably produce a damaged child. The therapy with this couple is ongoing and continues to be slow and painful, however, they are beginning to be able to use the sessions to think about their beliefs about themselves, their relationship and how their own disabilities came about.

People with learning disabilities as parents

Reproduction by people with learning disabilities has a controversial history. As noted in the introductory chapter, the Eugenics movement in the early twentieth century dictated that people with learning disabilities should not be allowed to reproduce because of the perceived danger of creating children with disabilities. Segregation and forced sterilisation have been documented; young women who gave birth to children out of wedlock were considered moral defectives and sent to institutions with their children put up for adoption.

More recently there have been debates in the media about whether people with learning disabilities should be allowed to have children and whether sterilisation is in their best interests. Some examples include the *Guardian* 19/05/2000, 'Appeal court bars sterilisation of woman with learning disabilities'; *Sunday Mail*, 19/03/2000, 'Abigail is thirteen and finding out about boys . . . now her mum wants her sterilised'; *Daily Telegraph*, 27/01/2000, 'Handicapped woman to lose womb without consent'; *Guardian*, 24/11/1999, 'Court asked to order vasectomy on Down's syndrome man'.

When people with learning disabilities do manage to have children the likelihood of being allowed to continue to parent them is poor. Research shows that 60 per cent of people with learning disabilities have their children taken into care compared with less than one per cent of the population without disabilities (Department of Health, 2000).

Sternfert-Kroese (2001) has studied attitudes to parents with learning disabilities and identified myths that exist and help to explain these disproportionate statistics. She found that people thought that children of parents with learning disabilities would also be learning disabled. In fact, the survey found that they were doing as well or better at school than others when matched for socio-economic status. Another attitude she found was an assumption that bad parenting is inevitable. The survey revealed that statistics relating to child abuse were lower among learning-disabled parents, that cases of neglect appear to be due to ignorance, and that with skills teaching, self-help manuals (for example, McGaw and Sturmey, 1994) and low-key support, parents with learning disabilities were shown to be competent and consistent in their parenting approach. Several other studies have supported these survey findings.

Research in the area of parenthood and people with learning disabilities is sparse and as most studies use clinical populations as participants the results of parenting outcomes is likely to be skewed. Booth and Booth (1994) note that parents with learning disabilities tend to be underrepresented in specialised services and that often the fact that a parent has learning disabilities only becomes evident when problems occur in the family. For example, a 5-year-old boy, Jack, was referred to the local children and family consultation service by the GP following continued complaints of behavioural problems at both home and school. It transpired that both parents had attended a local special school and had significant learning disabilities. The assessment revealed inconsistencies in the way the parents managed Jack's difficult behaviour. With guidance the family was helped to identify problem areas and Jack's behaviour calmed and became more manageable.

Booth and Booth (1994) highlight risk factors that increase the likelihood of child abuse and neglect including, deprivation, abuse or neglect in the parent's own childhood, low economic status and social isolation. These are all factors that are not uncommon in the population of people with learning disabilities.

In the account of family relationships above, it is clear that people with learning disabilities may be vulnerable to difficulties given their experience of being parented. Many of the examples in this volume illustrate the vulnerability of people with learning disabilities to social isolation.

Dowdney and Skuse (1993) stress there is no evidence to suggest that having a learning disability necessarily leads to inevitable poor parenting. Tymchuk and Andron (1994) found that IQ does not relate in any systematic way to parental competence until it falls below fifty-five to sixty. Parenting skills programmes have been found to be effective in helping people with learning disabilities to be 'good-enough' parents to their children (Llewellyn, 1994; Tymchuk, 1991). However, these findings need to be considered in the context of the important distinction made in psychodynamic therapy between cognitive intelligence and emotional intelligence. Regardless of cognitive ability, skills training does not work well when people experience obstacles to learning due to their personal and early history. In these cases longer-term psychotherapy might help to address such issues and overcome blocks to learning.

As the statistics above show, parents with learning disabilities are more likely to be without children than with them. Parenting has been a very significant role in their lives no matter how brief the actual experience has been.

CASE EXAMPLE: Sasha and Abby

Sasha is a thirty-year-old woman with mild learning disabilities. She was referred following a car accident that left her only able to walk using a walking stick. The referrer suggested counselling to help her to come to terms with her reduced mobility. However, even from her first counselling session she brought material that related to her experience of parenting and being parented.

Sasha had been in care from the age of five and despite efforts of the care staff Sasha's contact with her family diminished a few years after entering care. She had lived in a large

Continued

children's home and as a teenager had a brief relationship with a man and became pregnant: She had a daughter, Abby, when she was eighteen years old. Sasha had been offered an adult placement with a foster family who agreed to help her bring up the child. Sasha said that although the family had initially been kind and helpful, she found her foster mother suffocating; increasingly she went on drinking binges that resulted in violent outbursts at home. When Abby was three years old the placement broke down. Sasha described herself as 'losing it' and 'going off her rocker with the stress'. Abby's health visitor identified difficulties with her behaviour and social services became involved. Sasha was suicidal and was admitted to a psychiatric hospital. With no real support network there was no one to help look after Abby, who was fostered and eventually adopted.

Throughout the period of counselling Sasha's identity as a parent was paramount. It was particularly notable that at anniversaries (Abby's birthday, her own birthday), around breaks in therapy and when she experienced major setbacks, her angry feelings would manifest in the sessions. Sasha would become depressed and angry about her difficulty in walking. In talking about her need to prepare herself for the future and the possibility that Abby might try to contact her when she was older, Sasha made a comment that unconsciously revealed her feelings of damage 'I can't fill in the forms – I need to repair (prepare) myself'. The counsellor was able to link her anger and her wish to change her current situation with some of her past experiences. Issues of recurring loss and her anger at her own poor experiences of being parented, her mother leaving her when she was young and her having to enter a children's home aged five were slowly and carefully realised.

Sasha's counselling is ongoing, she continues to struggle with both the emotional and physical losses she has endured and she is very slowly using her sessions to begin to repair her very damaged and confusing internal world.

SUMMARY

- Early family relationships for people with learning disabilities can be difficult as parents struggle to come to terms with the birth of a disabled child. The literature suggests that many parents experience feelings of loss of the 'normal' baby they had hoped for and consequently mourning processes can interfere with the attachment and bonding processes.

- Later experiences can also prove problematic as families may re-experience feelings of loss, anger and bereavement with each transition that the person with learning disabilities makes.

- As a result of disrupted early experiences, lack of opportunities and difficulty in communication, making relationships outside the family can be difficult for people with learning disabilities.

- People with learning disabilities have the right to have sexual relationships; however, throughout history, intimate relationships between people with learning disabilities have been the centre of controversial debates. As a result people with learning disabilities have significantly reduced social networks and have been denied the right to sexual relationships and the experience of being parents.

- In addition to, and often as a result of, the traditional taboos of sex and disability, people with learning disabilities are likely to experience complex emotional reactions when faced with the possibility of intimate relationships.

- It is unknown how many people with learning disabilities are parents. Often they are not known to services unless difficulties occur. Research suggests that with adequate support people with learning disabilities have made 'good enough' parents to their children.

- There is an important role for psychodynamic counselling in helping people with learning disabilities to develop healthy and fulfilling relationships with their family members, their partners and their children.

7

RELATIONSHIP ISSUES: FRIENDSHIPS AND GROUP DYNAMICS

Nancy Sheppard

This chapter will focus on group dynamics and their relevance in understanding the relationships of people with learning disabilities. A group is defined by Barnes *et al.* (1999) as simply a collection of people who come together with a common aim. Once this boundary is created then the group becomes distinct from the non-group. Groups can have any chosen aim and the dynamics created by groups are evident in all groups, whether formal or informal. The first part of this chapter will explore some of the theories that have had a major influence on the understanding of group dynamics. The second part of the chapter will aim to explore the processes that can occur in the development and running of formal therapeutic groups. Finally, less formal group situations will be considered. Through discussing friendships and relationships that can develop within a group home the chapter will aim to explore how group dynamics can help understand difficulties that people with learning disabilities might experience in such informal relationships.

Theories of group dynamics

Two authors have had a profound impact on the understanding of behaviour in groups from a psychodynamic perspective: Bion and Foulkes.

Bion

Bion (1961) developed his thinking about the dynamics of groups whilst working on psychiatric wards in a military hospital during the Second World War, and then further refined his thoughts through his work at the Tavistock Clinic. He observed that certain patterns of behaviour would develop in different groups and drew on his knowledge of individual psychoanalysis to explain these patterns. Bion postulated that a boundary is needed for the group to exist but that this boundary also gives rise to the potential for both internal and external conflicts for the group. Bion suggests that there are two types of group: those that are pre-occupied with the primary task of the group or 'work mentality' groups, and those that work at avoiding the primary task or 'basic assumption' groups.

In a work mentality group there is space to discuss the primary task. All members are given adequate space for their views, there is room for new ideas to be proposed and explored in an even-handed way, responsibility is shared and the task is there-fore achieved. A work mentality will occur in any group, but Bion suggests that often group discussions following a work mental-ity will inevitably come up against difficulties and deteriorate into emotional states that are incompatible with achieving the group task. Bion named these different emotional states 'basic assump-tion mentality'. A basic assumption mentality group is one for whom the primary task evokes anxiety and highlights conflicts that occur within the group. Instead of working cooperatively to achieve this task the group works at avoiding the primary task and becomes preoccupied by what is happening in the group.

Bion suggests that these basic assumptions take three different forms, as described below. His theory is complex and is best illus-trated with examples. It should be noted that Bion developed his theory from his observations of formal group therapy, but argued that basic assumption mentality will be present in any group situation. The following examples are drawn from a variety of formal and informal groups for people with learning disabilities. The groups were not necessarily intended to be formal therapy groups but clearly illustrate group dynamics at work.

The basic assumption of dependency. The emotional state of the group is predominantly one of helplessness. The group relies on a leader who will concentrate on meeting the needs of the group members, for instance relieving anxiety from within the group and helping them to achieve the task.

CASE EXAMPLE: Adolescent group

This group was set up to think about difficulties young people were facing in leaving school and starting college or day centres. The group task was clearly anxiety provoking for all the group members – not only were they facing the challenges of adolescence and leaving school but they experienced additional challenges relating to their learning disabilities.

The group had been talking about their free bus passes that were being renewed in the next week. One of the counsellors observed that of the six group members, four had replaced the orange wallet issued with the card for a leather one or a different coloured one (black or white) and commented that the orange wallet showed other people that the pass was free. There was a painful silence and the group members looked towards the other counsellor, who in turn, felt an overwhelming need to say something to rescue the group from the painful realisation of their disability and difference from other people. She commented on this countertransference feeling. Eventually Joshua, the most able group member, looked round the four and said, 'Well, you know, the orange ones break, they rip like this, here (pointing to the seam of the wallet) they are no good. Helen's leather one and these others don't break so easy'. The group then began to talk about the relative merits of their wallets over the orange ones. The counsellors recognised that the group had found the idea of thinking about the orange wallets that identified them as people with learning disabilities as extremely anxiety provoking. The group had looked to the counsellor to rescue them and to help them avoid thinking about this. Having not found their rescuer in the counsellor they were extremely grateful to Joshua who had readily led them away from the anxiety provoking reality and thought of other reasons why they might need different, less labelling, bus pass wallets.

The basic assumption of flight or fight. Here the group is dominated by feelings of aggression, anger or fear. Group members help to channel these difficult feelings by trying to organise a leader who will generate enemies from outside the group. The hope is that the leader will then lead the members in the task of fighting or concentrate on fights within the group. Alternatively conflict and anxiety might be avoided by not attending the group (flight).

CASE EXAMPLE: Day centre group

The basic assumption, fight or flight group was evident in a current affairs group for people with learning disabilities and additional physical disabilities held in a day centre. Leon had arrived at the group without the tray for his wheelchair. He asked if he could go and get it so that he could participate in reading the newspapers with the group. He has some difficulty in walking and was unable to go to get it himself without the assistance of the group facilitator. One of the group facilitators offered to go and fetch it for him and left the room. In her absence, Leon became very angry, saying that his key-worker had left it behind but he should be allowed to go and get it. He said he hated the workers at the day centre and the group facilitators. He said that the group was a waste of his time, he could be doing an IT class instead that would help him to get a job. He remained angry and aggressive throughout the group session. The whole group began to talk about their difficulties with the staff at the day centre. In the previous group session there had been some discussion about disability and handicap and the facilitators linked this to Leon's angry outburst. One facilitator commented that Leon's wish to go and get his tray might have suddenly made his own difficulty in walking very real. The pain of this reality made Leon and the rest of the group extremely anxious. Leon reacted initially by wanting to leave the group. However, when he was unable to leave (or take flight) the group became a fighting faction against the able-bodied day centre workers.

Basic assumption of pairing. The group is preoccupied with feelings of optimism and anticipation, the members focus on uniting in intense relationships or pairs (both in and outside the group) in hope of creating a positive future for the group.

CASE EXAMPLE: Women's group

The basic assumption mentality (pairing) is illustrated in a session taken from a group for women with mild learning disabilities, run by two facilitators. In the previous session the group had been talking about relationships with men and had touched on the subject of sexual relationships. They had begun to explore their past experiences of sexual relationships and had started to come to the painful realisation that none of them had ever experienced an equal, loving relationship. Julie began to tell the group that her social worker had taken her to visit a flat that she was planning to move into in a supported living scheme. Fatima, already living in the scheme, joined in the conversation and the facilitators noticed that the other group members appeared to be listening attentively. The conversation continued throughout the session with Julie and Fatima exchanging plans for decorating their flats and talking about activities they might do together once Julie moved in. Any attempts for the facilitators to bring other members into the discussion appeared to be ignored. At the end of the session the facilitators were both left feeling hopeless. They had been encouraged in a previous meeting that the women were finally talking about issues that they hoped would be addressed by the group and felt frustrated that the discussion about relationships had not continued. In their supervision session they explored this feeling further and agreed that the previous group discussion had provoked extreme anxiety in the group members. There had been no opportunity for this anxiety to be addressed as the group session time was up. The group was relieved that Julie and Fatima had brought an issue that allowed them to avoid thinking about the painful issue of intimate, reciprocal relationships and they had unconsciously adopted a basic assumption mentality whereby the pairing between Julie and Fatima acted as a means to avoid the possibility of returning to the topic of relationships.

Foulkes

Foulkes (1948, 1964) saw group dynamics somewhat differently to Bion. In developing a theory of group analysis, he drew both on insights into individual personality from Freudian psychoanalytic thought and on social psychology, which explores the relationships between individuals. Foulkes understood individuals' behaviour in the therapeutic group as a mirror of their experiences in the world outside the group, for instance, experiences in the family group.

CASE EXAMPLE: Helen and Margaret

Helen, who had recently joined a therapy group for people with learning disabilities, arrived ten minutes late and sat down in the only empty chair. After a short silence, John asked Helen what had happened to make her late; she didn't answer, but blushed and looked flustered. Margaret started to talk about the difficulties she had with her support workers arriving late to her flat to help her with her personal care, which has made her late for appointments before. Helen sank lower into her chair and was very quiet. The group facilitator commented on Helen's embarrassment. Helen started to cry. Margaret then got upset when she saw Helen crying and said that she only meant she was also late for things sometimes. Later in the group it became clear that Helen's older sister had always complained and shouted at Helen to hurry up and not be late. The group's comments on Helen's lateness brought back her early experiences and she transferred her difficult relationship with her sister onto Margaret, making her potentially supportive comments seem accusatory.

In the group analysis approach, transference is considered important at several levels: relationships; the transference to the counsellor; the transference relationships with other members of the group; and transference to other relationships the individual has outside the group. Foulkes believed a group could have therapeutic benefit to the participants if the group facilitator is able to observe and keep in mind both the individual's thoughts and feelings and the processes of the group as a whole.

It is these basic principles that make up much of the theory of group behaviour today. The dynamics within a group can be present regardless of the type of group described, they will exist in formal therapy groups as strongly as between the residents living together in a group home or in relationships between friends.

Formal groups

Trowell (1995) notes that Foulkes's group analysis methodology is appropriate and well suited to groups run by workers with basic training in group dynamics, because conductors can avoid the destructive elements of groups that Bion's theory of group dynamics requires. When working with very vulnerable groups, however, Trowell suggests that the very early, unprocessed dynamics described by Bion are more likely to be in play. This can result in immense pressure on group facilitators in terms of having to bear and make sense of the painful projections from group members. However, it is vital that the group conductor remains thoughtful and can survive these projections in order to help the group members to come to terms with some of the painful processes. In both models supervision from a trained group analyst is a necessary requirement in considering group facilitation of formal groups. It can also be extremely helpful and is highly recommended as a means of helping workers explore group dynamics in less formal group situations.

There is a growing body of published work about working with people with learning disabilities in psychotherapeutic and psychoanalytic groups, for example Pantlin (1985), Hollins and Evered (1990) Hollins (1992), O'Connor (2001). In all of these papers group dynamics are discussed. Pantlin (1985) talks about the difficulties his group had in starting the group. He felt that the group members' persistence in being 'slow on the uptake' was a defensive means of keeping thinking at bay in the early stages of his group. Hollins and Evered (1990) found that initially their group had a disjointed feel, with members talking over one another, and there was a strong sense of competition for attention between group members. They expanded Pantlin's idea that the initial defensiveness of refusing to think was exacerbated by the belief that others would not expect them to think. Hollins and Evered found that group cohesion improved when the group began to talk about being labelled as handicapped. The group was able to find common ground and a unity in the feeling of 'it hurting inside' and seemed to find a supportive defensiveness in sticking together.

The task of the group counsellor is to notice when themes such as handicap, loss and difference are brought up within the group discussion and to acknowledge them with careful interpretations. The aim of the group is to help each other address issues in a contained and safe place so that difficult and painful feelings can be thought about. It is hoped that by revealing hidden conflicts the group members will experience a decrease in secondary handicap symptoms, will be better able to express themselves in terms of their emotions and feelings, and will begin the process of reparation of their sense of being incomplete and different.

Other groups for people with learning disabilities

Groups have traditionally been a popular way of working with people with learning disabilities. Aveline and Dryden (1988) argue that too often groupwork is viewed as an inferior substitute for individual work. They suggest reasons for this unfavourable comparison have grown from the misguided assumptions that working with groups of individuals provides an economical means of spreading workers' limited time to a number of recipients, and that groupwork might be a means of avoiding contact with people who could be seen as difficult to work with or considered too difficult to use individual therapy. Given the devalued status of people with learning disabilities and the poorly resourced services that they have traditionally received, this comparison may be a realistic one and could offer a plausible explanation to the predominance of group interventions with this population. However, groupwork with both children and adults has been shown to be beneficial in terms of both therapeutic outcome and as a cost effective use of staff time (Sant Angelo *et al.*, 2001; Bender *et al.*, 1992).

Groups might have a range of aims to help people with particular problems or to help people tackle particular life changes that they might be facing, for instance, therapeutic groups for anger management, relaxation, anxiety management, bereavement, art therapy, music therapy, drama therapy and social skills groups or communication skills groups.

Groups have been used as a means of helping people with learning disabilities by raising awareness of relevant issues, for instance, educational awareness groups such as health promotion, sex education, personal development, HIV and aids, health and fitness. On a more political level they have also been used to motivate people to advocate or speak up for themselves; for instance, self advocacy groups such as People First, Power House, Black People First, while they have also been useful in addressing the difficulties associated with belonging to a de-valued group of citizens as, for instance, consciousness raising groups. Szivos and Griffiths (1992) describe how groupwork and group processes can help people with learning disabilities challenge their stigmatised identity. The notion of consciousness raising as a means of helping people with learning disabilities has grown out of criticism of the 'Normalisation Principle' (Wolfensberger, 1972). Szivos and Griffiths (1992) note that 'passing for normal', the aim of normalisation, has unwanted psychological and social consequences. People may feel ashamed that they belong to a devalued group, the notion that the stigmatised group is inferior to the dominant group is perpetuated and there could be devastating consequences for those members of the stigmatised group who do not succeed in 'passing'. Szivos and Griffiths (1992) look to the experience of other stigmatised groups (women, homosexuals, and people from minority ethnic groups) and aim to use a process of consciousness raising as a means of exploring the stigmatised identity in order to help people with learn-ing disabilities gain strength by developing a positive group identity.

Issues pertinent in setting up groups for people with learning disabilities

Barnes *et al.* (1999) discuss three issues that group facilitators should consider themselves in planning a group:

- Who do you want to help? (The participants of the group)
- What do you want to achieve? (The purpose of the group)
- How can you achieve this purpose for this group of people? (The type of group)

For further, detailed information about how to set up and run formal group analytic therapy see Barnes *et al.* (1999); there are, however, some issues that need particular attention when considering a group for people with learning disabilities.

Authority to set up a group

People with learning disabilities, by nature of their disabilities, will often need support to lead an ordinary life. As a result, they will inevitably be part of a large system of caregivers. In making a decision to provide a group or group therapy experience for people with learning disabilities, it is particularly important to gain authority from all parties involved in order to ensure the group will develop and run smoothly.

The setting

As with all therapeutic interventions of a psychodynamic nature, it is important to provide a safe space for the group to take place and to observe the boundaries of the group clearly and precisely. In order to achieve this aim the group should take place in the same room at the same time each week. Ground rules and boundaries will vary according to the function and purpose of the group, however, it is particularly important with participants who have learning disabilities to explain clearly at the beginning of a group why boundaries are important and to make sure that ground rules set are fully understood.

Participants

Issues relating to assessing people for individual counselling are discussed in detail in Chapter 3. All of these points are equally valid and important when considering whether a group therapy approach will be helpful for the individual. There are, however, some additional factors that should be carefully considered both in thinking about the individual participants and how the group as a whole might function. In Chapter 3 it is stressed that a degree of preserved emotional intelligence allows an individual to engage in a therapeutic relationship. It is particularly important to make a careful and thorough assessment of emotional intelligence when considering an individual for group therapy because, as Foulkes's work illustrates, the transference relationships present in group dynamics can be very powerful.

Another important consideration for counsellors proposing a group for people with learning disabilities is to assess the group as a whole in order to avoid potentially difficult or devastating dynamics developing. The range of abilities within the group should be balanced and it is important to ensure that no one participant is markedly different from the group as a whole. For example, Hernadez-Halton (personal communication) discusses some difficulties that arose in a group for women with learning disabilities. All of the group participants had mild to moderate leaning disabilities, however, only one woman had Down's syndrome, making her the only group member to be visibly different from the rest of the group. The group facilitators found that over the course of the group the participants consistently projected difficult feelings about their own disabilities into the woman with Down's syndrome. The group therapists were able to address these issues within the boundaries of the group and the woman clearly had the ego strength to manage the projections, however, with less experienced therapists the situation could have been potentially more damaging than beneficial for that particular group member and the group as a whole.

Confidentiality

Often people with learning disabilities living in one borough or district will know one another through different contexts, and therefore may have some shared history through living together in group homes, hostels or hospitals, attending the same school, day centre or sheltered work project. Even if they do not have any setting in common the fact that most people will have used specialist services at one point in their lives may mean that they have relationships with certain professionals in other contexts. In one group run for adults with learning disabilities within a local community team for people with learning disabilities, five group members out of seven had had contact with the local Learning Disabilities Consultant Psychiatrist. Once the group had established this through one member talking about his experience of medication, other members voiced concern about what they had said and whether it would somehow get back to the Consultant Psychiatrist. Hollins (1992) discusses additional difficulties that arise in confidentiality when running a group for people with learning disabilities due to their dependency on services and how the counsellor might communicate with care givers.

Informal groups and friendships

It is well documented that social relationships and friendships are important factors contributing to a person's overall psychological well-being and a good quality of life (Schalock, 1996). Richardson and Ritchie (1989) explored the quality of friendships in people with learning disabilities and found that friendship provides company, intimacy or emotional support and practical help. Friendships can help individuals to value themselves, gain pleasure and support in difficult situations and gain positive feedback from others that, in turn, can increase self worth, self esteem and confidence.

Historically people with learning disabilities have had extremely restricted social networks (Robertson et al., 2001). Segregation and isolation meant there were few opportunities to meet people. In hospital settings social relationships were described as most frequently occurring with paid members of staff, and studies rarely comment on peer relationships or friendships (Markova et al., 1992).

Studies such as Emerson and Hatton (1994) and Flynn (1989) suggest that moving people from institutional care into community care and supported living has increased the number of contacts that, on average, a person with learning disabilities has. However, interviews and qualitative research exploring the content of these contacts show that they tend to be contacts with people providing services (for example shop owners) or, more frequently, visits from relatives. Few people have increased their circle of informal support or friendships with non-disabled peers. Yet the quality of life of people living in community residential settings is largely determined by the range and type of their social relationships (Sheppard, 1991). The full range of social relationships, from acquaintances to intimate friends, is less likely to be

a reality for people with learning disabilities and research suggests that reciprocal relationships are also uncommon. (Newland,
1996, personal communication).

The role of friends in an individual's life is varied but they can
often be a source of emotional support in decision making, in
times of trouble and in times of stress by taking up an informal
counselling or advice-giving role. Jobling *et al.* (2000) suggest that
without friends, life can become increasingly lonely, and where
the roles of 'counsellor' or 'emotional support' are absent, a person's psychosocial quality of life can be affected.

Following changes in policy, such as the White Paper 'Valuing
People' (2001) services have been developing life planning systems and supported living projects that aim to draw on communities to support individuals and to involve informal sources
of support much more than in the past. It has been argued that
informal support and support coming from many sources rather
than a few paid carers and professionals reduces dependency in
people with learning disabilities (O'Brien, 1987). However, there
still appear to be difficulties in moving from acquaintance to
friendship. Frith and Rapley (1990) have tried to identify barriers
that people with learning disabilities experience in developing
friendships: people with disabilities are significantly less likely
than a non-disabled comparison group to go to discos, cinema or
to be spectators or participants in sporting or physical activities.
In addition, activities tend to be home and family based and
the more severe the disability the less likely the person is to
be involved in leisure activities. Another barrier to developing
friendships was identified as a lack of money. People with learning disabilities tend to belong to groups with low socio-economic
status due to unemployment and reliance on benefits and therefore have little disposable income to spend on socialising and
leisure pursuits. Landesman-Dwyer and Berkson (1984) showed
that larger institutions or residences appeared to facilitate
social relationships whilst those people living in smaller homes
reported loneliness and social isolation. This may be linked to the
fact that reliance on non-disabled people to transport, escort and
supervise activities is also likely to constrain access to leisure
activities (Frith and Rapley, 1990).

In addition to the practical barriers that may prevent people
with learning disabilities from meeting potential friends, there

are also likely to be emotional barriers to making relationships. People with learning disabilities may have experienced a number of rejecting relationships in the past and poor role models in relationships, such as over-protective relationships fostering dependency, and controlling and impersonal relationships with paid carers. In terms of group dynamics this may leave them particularly vulnerable to not making lasting relationships. Complex past relationships are as likely to be relived in a transference relationship with a potential friend as they are within the formal group setting. However, without the boundaries of the group and the insight of the group counsellor such dynamics are more likely to have a negative effect on the relationship and result in relationship breakdowns.

By the nature of their learning disability, people are likely to have difficulties in both expressing themselves articulately, in understanding others and in reading situations. When asked about her friendships, one young woman with moderate learning disabilities and autistic traits said that she knew the library assistant wanted to be her friend because of his shoes and his haircut. She was not able to give any information about anything the library assistant had said or done to suggest a desire for a friendship to develop.

Other barriers to developing friendships include low self-esteem and a lack of confidence in approaching other people. Segregation of services not only leads to a further lack of opportunities to mix with people without learning disabilities, but also adds to the stigma of being associated with a devalued group; this could further reduce self esteem and confidence. The case example below describes a group run for young people with learning disabilities and shows how some of these barriers can impact on the participants. The group described also explores some of the meanings that the members attached to their friendships. There is little literature that elicits the views of people with learning disabilities with regard to the meaning of friendships. Knox and Hickson (2001) examined the views of four people with learning disabilities on the relationships in their lives, which they described as close friendships. The four participants distinguished 'good mates' from 'intimate relationships' (girlfriend or boyfriend). The authors extracted several themes linked to the concept of 'good mates' from the participants' narratives: being an important friend or having a pivotal relationship, doing lots of things together or being a pervasive part of the participant's life, growing up together or having a sense of a shared history, sharing common interests, helping each other and maintaining the relationship through keeping to arrangements and balancing other relationships. Some of these themes are reflected in the example of the group below.

CASE EXAMPLE: Trevor and Frank

Trevor and Frank were both members of a therapeutic group set up for young people with mild to moderate learning disabilities. Trevor was twenty-five years old and lived with his uncle and aunt. He attended an employment project twice a week and went shopping with his uncle once a week. Trevor was referred to the group following several violent outbursts and aggressive behaviour towards his carers. During the course of the group it became clear that Trevor's aggression was related to increasing resentment towards his uncle for not allowing him to go out and meet people. His uncle's view was that when he did go out he was vulnerable to a local group of children who had taunted him on his way home from college.

Frank was nineteen and lived with his parents and siblings. He had been diagnosed as having mild learning disabilities and had attended mainstream school. He had had a small group of friends from his school but they had all left the area either to attend further education or for employment reasons. Since leaving school Frank had been unemployed and had started to spend time with a group of local boys. It was clear from his descriptions of the gang's activities that the other members were very aware of Frank's difficulties and were using him to take the blame in situations where there was trouble. As a result, Frank was arrested for two minor offences; the charges were dropped when his parents appealed and his learning disability was revealed.

Both these young men were restricted in their friendships. Both talked in the group about what they expected from friends, including loyalty, as in someone who will stick with you if things get bad; respect, namely, someone who likes you and looks up to you; and someone who shared their interests, for instance, someone to do things with and who knows things you might want to do. Through group counselling both Trevor and Frank were able to think about their expectations in terms of their current relationships. In one moving session Frank said that since he got into trouble he recognised that his 'friends' were not true friends. He said it scared him but he knew that they had used him because he was not as smart as they were. He said this made him feel angry and very sad because it meant he had no real friends now. Trevor, on the other hand, had very little contact with people outside of his family. Each week at the end of the group he would check that he had the other group members' telephone numbers and said he would phone them and arrange to meet between group sessions. He never did and would make an excuse about having to help his uncle. Frank, the most able group member, found this very difficult to accept and would tease Trevor by asking him what he was doing to be so busy! Trevor struggled with this challenge and became irritated and shouted that his uncle wouldn't let him use the phone anyway. Over the duration of the group it became possible for Trevor to admit that he could not phone them as he did not know how to use a phone and could not read the numbers that he wrote down each week. Following this revelation Frank suggested he ask his uncle to help. Trevor did, and telephoned a group member that week.

Living in a group home

An estimated 37 per cent of adults with learning disabilities live in residential communal care. The ratio of people living in private households decreases with age; for instance, only 30 per cent of 20–24 year olds live in communal residential establishments, while by age 55 over 70 per cent of people with learning disabilities share their homes with their peers rather than family members (Kavanagh and Opit, 1999). It is notable that for people in similar age groups without disabilities the trend is reversed.

Over the past thirty years there has been a significant change in the type of residential care services provided for people with learning disabilities, from large institutions to smaller group homes, hostels and supported living schemes. Most residential establishments are underpinned with the philosophy of normalisation or providing services that pertain to achieving an ordinary life (Wolfensberger, 1972). O'Brien (1987) derived five achievable 'Service Accomplishments' from the principle of normalisation which aim to offer service users with services that promote choice, community presence, competence, community participation and respect. There is considerable evidence that the move to provision of smaller, community services has been beneficial for people with learning disabilities (Kim *et al.*, 2001). In reality, however, people with learning disabilities have rarely chosen whom they live with and services are often designed according to economic restraints rather than the individual's needs. As a result the dynamics that develop between residents in communal homes can cause difficulties in group relationships.

CASE EXAMPLE: Chris, Tina and Billy

Chris was a thirty-five-year-old man with moderate learning disabilities and Down's syndrome. He lived with Tina and Billy in a group home with twenty-four hour support by a small staff team. Chris's key worker, George, felt that he was suffering from a difficult bereavement reaction following the death of his mother five years previously. George wrote to the Learning Disabilities service with a request for bereavement counselling for Chris.

During an initial assessment session some complex group dynamics came to light. Chris and Billy had lived together for many years, moving to the home from a local Learning Disabilities Hospital. Tina had moved into the house six months previously, when Frankie moved out to a supported living scheme. Since Tina's arrival, Chris had been tearful and spent long periods of time in his room refusing to be involved in group activities. Staff felt that Tina and Chris got on well but were concerned that Tina's mother visited the house every Sunday and that this might be upsetting Chris. They were also surprised because Chris and Billy had both found Frankie difficult to live with, as she was more able than they were and often shouted and told them what to do. Following the assessment Chris was offered individual bereavement counselling to address some of his feelings, especially the loss of his mother and the complicated feelings about losing Frankie. However, during several feedback sessions with the staff, it was possible to address some of the wider group dynamics that the counsellor experienced with the residents. Chris and Billy's difficult relationship with Frankie and Chris's withdrawal from the group activities in the face of change could be understood in terms of Bion's basic assumption of fight or flight. It was also helpful for the staff to think further about Chris's reaction to Tina's arrival and her relationship with her mother in terms of a transference of his relationship to his own mother. He had become quickly attached to Tina as a mother figure, but found the painful reality of the loss of his mother difficult when he watched Tina with hers.

SUMMARY

- Bion (1961) and Foulkes (1964) developed theories of group dynamics that are helpful in understanding group processes in both formal and informal group situations.
- Literature describing formal group therapy with people with learning disabilities has highlighted a number of recurrent themes that emerged from group discussions, namely, disability, death and mortality, dependency and sexuality. These themes are consistent with Sinason's (1992) 'tasks of therapy'.
- Informal groupwork has been a popular and effective means of working with people with learning disabilities. Groups have been used to teach practical skills, impart important information regarding health issues, raise awareness, provide support and help people with learning disabilities overcome specific difficulties.

- Issues pertinent in setting up groupwork with people with learning disabilities include: gaining relevant permission or authority to set up the group, choice of setting and establishing clear boundaries, making careful assessments of individuals to ensure they will benefit from a group experience and making issues of confidentiality clear to all parties involved.
- People with learning disabilities may experience difficulties in developing friendships. Barriers to making friends include lack of opportunity and restricted social networks, dependency on others, difficulty in accessing leisure activities, financial restraints, difficulties with communication and emotional blocks in developing lasting relationships.
- Application of group dynamics to informal group relationships, for example friendships and living in group homes, can help develop deeper understanding of the emotional processes at play and can help to explain difficult behaviour in these situations.

8

WORKING WITH CARE STAFF AND ORGANISATIONS

Nancy Sheppard

The main body of this book has explored how a psychodynamic counselling approach can offer individuals with learning disabilities an opportunity to gain a deeper understanding of their emotional difficulties and to develop emotional maturity. However, individual counselling for people with learning disabilities is a rare resource, not least in the current NHS climate where face-to-face contacts and short 'episodes of care' are highly valued and longer-term work is not seen as 'best value' (Department of Health, 2001).

An alternative intervention is for the counsellor to work with a staff group. The process of staff consultation aims to help staff develop a better understanding of client's emotional lives. This chapter will expand on some of the issues discussed previously, and will look specifically at the dynamics of relationships within staff groups who work with people with learning disabilities. I aim to explore how psychodynamic ideas can be used to support staff in different ways, through encouraging understanding in the dynamics of escorting individuals with learning disabilities to their therapy, by offering direct consultation and supervision to staff groups, and finally by exploring how psychodynamic ideas can help in developing effective training packages for staff groups.

Residential care workers

Currently an estimated 37 per cent of people with learning disabilities live in accommodation supported by paid members of staff (Kavanagh and Opit, 1999). Support services range from 'supported living' where staff visit people living independently for a fixed number of hours per week to help with, for example, budgeting, shopping and domestic or personal care tasks, to twenty-four-hour staffed homes where people rely on staff to help them with all activities of daily living. A wide range of organisations exist to provide this care, including those run by health services, social services, voluntary and private agencies. Therefore, people with learning disabilities are likely to be involved with numerous care providing agencies and individuals.

CASE EXAMPLE: Lucy's network of workers

Lucy lives by herself. She is thirty years old with moderate learning disabilities. Lucy can be very challenging to those who care for her and she requires a one-to-one ratio of staff support. Three care workers, one deputy manager and a manager staff the house. Lucy's house is owned by a housing association and her care staff are provided by a large care-giving organisation. Lucy's parents live nearby and she visits them on a weekly basis. She has two brothers who she visits every two months. When she was twenty years old Lucy was admitted to an acute psychiatric inpatient unit following an episode of disturbed behaviour when she destroyed property and was verbally and physically aggressive to her parents with whom she was then living. Lucy found her stay at the inpatient unit very difficult to cope with and her parents felt that they were no longer able to care for her at home. It was felt important to introduce Lucy to a citizen advocate to help make decisions about her future care. Gina, the citizen advocate, has continued to be involved in Lucy's life on a regular basis. Lucy has an allocated care manager from the local authority and attends two day centres; she has a key worker in both. Due to her challenging behaviour the manager and deputy manager of both day centres have regular meetings with the home manager and the residential service manager. Lucy suffers from epilepsy and makes regular visits to her GP and a consultant neurologist at the local hospital; a community learning disabilities nurse supports these visits.

Lucy attends weekly counselling sessions with a counsellor. The Learning Disabilities Consultant Psychiatrist regularly reviews her medication. A clinical psychologist provides monthly consultation sessions for Lucy's care staff team.

Lucy has a relationship with a man with mild learning disabilities, she has regular contact with a friend living nearby, goes to the local pub regularly in the evenings, attends People First Meetings and a Gateway club.

This example illustrates how, although Lucy has a busy life with many social engagements, of the twenty-four people she sees regularly, seventeen of these people are paid members of staff and are providing her with a service.

There is a large volume of literature relating to work with staff who offer direct support to people with learning disabilities. Much of this literature comprises studies exploring the relationship between staff stress levels and challenging behaviour. Sharrard (1992) notes that stress is one of the most important factors, as staff under stress will be less able to undertake their duties to the best of their abilities. Sources of stress can include poorly defined roles and consequent role ambiguity for staff, the characteristics of the people being cared for, including challenging behaviour and violence, and pressure from management (Rose, 1995). Another important factor that Rose highlights is that staff reported lower stress levels when they felt well supported by colleagues and their immediate managers. He cites evidence of a highly significant correlation between stress levels and reported social support in staff teams (Raynes *et al.*, 1990).

Issues relating to retention and recruitment of staff to residential services for people with learning disabilities have also been explored. Hatton *et al.* (1995) highlight that most staff working in residential services for people with learning disabilities in the UK are young females with no professional qualifications. Rose (1995) cites several studies that have shown that staff turnover in community residential services is between 5 and 48 per cent. Researchers have aimed to identify factors that explain this wide range of figures by looking at job satisfaction and 'burn out'. Factors identified include: economic rewards, possibilities for promotion or a career path, client characteristics, management styles, size of work unit, opportunities for personal development and training, role ambiguity, role conflict and work load (Zaharia and Baumeister, 1979; Razza, 1993; Dyer and Quinn, 1998).

Hastings (1998) investigates staff attitudes and emotional reactions to challenging behaviour and concludes that providing training for staff helps to modify attitudes. After training, staff were less likely to attribute challenging behaviours to personality traits and more likely to consider environmental factors in assessing reasons for challenging behaviour occurring.

Goble (1999) explored people with learning disabilities' perceptions of staff and services. Three major themes emerged from unstructured interviews with seven people with mild to moderate learning disabilities. The participants talked about the physical presence and absence of staff: the emotional impact of interactions with staff and the political impact of their interactions with staff, that is, what changes happened in their lives as a result of interactions.

There is less literature that examines some of the issues underlying these factors relating to staff working with people with learning disabilities (Thomas, 2001; Symington, 1992). For instance, what is it about working with people with challenging behaviour that makes it so stressful? What are the components of staff training that enable staff to change their attitudes towards the service users they are working with? How does role conflict develop? A psychodynamic approach can lend considerable understanding to these factors and help to understand how the work impacts on the staff and how the staff impact on the organisation.

Zagier-Roberts (1998) illustrates complex organisational dynamics using a case example of a group of staff providing residential care for a group of people with profound learning disabilities. She discusses the dilemmas encountered by the director of the service that emerged during individual consultation sessions. She describes how, whenever positive changes took place and there seemed to be hope for the future of the organisation, a crisis would occur and chaos ensued. Zagier-Roberts and the director concluded that the dynamics underlying this demoralising pattern were that the work with this group was unbearable for the staff group, and that the project that seemed to be the focus for much of the chaos was a house set up for a group of five of the most disabled, disturbed and frequently violent individuals. The director came to believe that this group was unsuitably placed and perhaps should not have been housed together. In fact, with hindsight, they may have been happier and more appropriately placed in the hospital setting that they had left in order to live in the project. Zagier-Roberts suggests that it was by admitting this painful finding, that was so out of synchrony with both her personal philosophy and the philosophy of the organisation, that the director could see what action was needed.

Menzies (1959) applied knowledge gained from providing group therapy to organisations, and noticed how anxieties generated by working on the core task of the organisation gave rise to institutional defences revealed through the practices and structures observed in the organisation. These defences build up essentially as a means of avoiding the anxiety related to the task, and can therefore create barriers to staff performing tasks effectively and appropriately (a process described in detail in Chapter 7). In any consultation role it is important to gain knowledge about the organisation, the staff roles within the organisation and to begin to identify the attitudes and feelings towards the organisation, and the client group that might manifest through the staff's behaviour, practices and how they talk about their work. This is because often the feelings present within the staff team mirror feelings about the organisation, feelings towards the clients and feelings that the clients may have themselves.

Providing consultation to staff groups can be very useful in helping address these issues. However, most referrals relate to requests for individuals rather than work with staff. How and when to offer staff consultation to staff groups can be vital in successful consultations. In considering how best to introduce the possibility of a consultation package it has been helpful to think about Rustin's (1998) model of working with parents. She suggests that there are different levels of work with parents of children in individual therapy and that these different levels are possible and necessary according to where the parents of the children are in their own internal world. Rustin suggests that therapists working with parents need to carefully assess the parents' capacity to engage in a therapeutic relationship, but when the work begins, the relationship with the counsellor affords opportunities to internalise stronger and more sustaining experiences. This allows parents to become both more realistic and more hopeful in facing the painful struggle to help their children to develop to the best of their potential. When an assessment suggests that difficulties might lie with the dynamics within a staff group rather than directly with an individual, it is important to assess how best the group might be helped by a consultation approach. Rustin's different levels provide a useful model to assess the ability of staff to enter into a helping relationship. There are several ways in which a psychodynamic model might help to address difficulties the staff are experiencing in their work.

- supporting staff to allow individual therapy to take place;
- consulting with staff groups to help them to think about the roles they take in the lives of people with learning disabilities;
- teaching staff groups through training courses, for instance, working positively with people with challenging behaviour, working with people with learning disabilities around issues of bereavement, and making transitions.

Supporting staff to allow therapy to take place

Clients who do not show up on time, do not attend appointments after breaks or attend appointments during scheduled breaks, come to the wrong office or even to the wrong building, escorts who ask 'how was she today?' and engage in a conversation about the journey to the clinic, making complaints that the client is always worse after the therapy session, are all things that can happen on a regular basis. At best this can cause difficulties in the therapeutic relationship that need to be addressed and at worst have resulted in the counselling relationship breaking down. There is very little written about the role of escorts and staff in supporting therapy, yet it is a vital role in allowing a therapeutic counselling relationship to begin and to be sustained.

CASE EXAMPLE: Working with Colin's care staff

A colleague working with a man with moderate learning disabilities and severe challenging behaviour asked for some help in working with the staff team supporting him. Colin was regularly brought to his sessions either late or too early. Mark, my colleague, would often be asked questions about the counselling and whether Colin had been 'good' or not. Mark was anxious to keep his therapeutic boundaries with Colin clear and as a result wished to avoid engaging in conversation with the escorts who brought Colin to his sessions. Staff, however, complained that Mark was being rude to them by not engaging in conversation with them, for example when they asked if he had had a nice holiday following a break. In addition, there were two incidents where Colin became very challenging, shouting, swearing, and threatening to hit the escort in the waiting room. On both occasions Colin had arrived very early for his appointment and had had to wait a long time in the waiting room. When Mark was called to help deal with the situation, Colin immediately calmed down and went into his session as if nothing had happened. The staff found this experience very frightening and were questioning whether they could continue to support the counselling. Mark was very clear that Colin was using the sessions well and that overall his challenging behaviour had decreased since counselling had begun. The staff agreed that a consultation with a clinical psychologist would be helpful and a meeting was arranged.

Negotiating the consultation role in this case was vital as the consultant was aware that the request had come from her colleague and not the staff group. Initially a meeting with the home manager was arranged in order to establish expectations of the intervention and to negotiate a contract with the staff team. In the meeting with the manager the positive outcomes of the counselling and the staff's recognition that they needed help in supporting the therapy were discussed. It was agreed that the consultant's role would be to explain the counselling process and to explore ways of giving staff greater 'ownership' and understanding of the counselling process. It was also

Continued

agreed that the consultant would be prepared to offer regular meetings to help think about the effects of the changes in Colin's behaviour as a result of the counselling sessions.

The staff group were all female, aged between 20 and 50. The consultation took place in a relatively neutral place for the staff, away from their workplace.

In explaining the counselling process, the consultant gave examples of transference, countertransference and projection and incorporated Bion's ideas about containing and containment. These ideas were made relevant to the staff team by translating them into everyday experiences that the staff group might have had. For instance, the experience of having feelings of resentment building up over the course of one day at work and then going home and finding oneself shouting at one's husband, partner or best friend for something one would normally be very tolerant about, or the experience of finding oneself repeatedly engaging in certain patterns of behaviour and how this might relate to past experiences. The staff engaged in a discussion about the issues that arose from the examples and they were helped to relate these ideas to some of the difficulties that Colin might be experiencing.

The staff reported that they found the session helpful and asked if they could have regular meetings to continue to think about Colin and his behaviour towards them in this way. Mark reported that Colin tended to arrive on time more regularly and that if he did not come either he or a carer would telephone to leave a message. There were occasional hitches when bank staff or new staff were on duty, but during the regular support meetings the staff group brought an individual plan that they had developed with Colin to help let new staff know how best to work with him. This included a section on Colin's sessions with Mark and gave advice about how to help Colin to get to his counselling, both emotionally and physically.

Consultation to staff groups

Obholzer and Zagier-Roberts (1994) looked at the process of consultation and working with vulnerable groups. They noted that working with vulnerable people in a helping profession is stressful. People with learning disabilities, due to the nature of their disabilities and society's perception of disability and difference, are likely to have experienced traumatic separations and transitions, are vulnerable to abuse, and may struggle to negotiate and understand difficult life experiences, leaving them in great emotional pain. Being in close contact with such pain leads to both conscious and unconscious anxieties and these anxieties contribute to feelings of stress.

Halton (1994) suggests it is a difficult task to identify the sources of anxiety in an organisation. In individual therapy with children, for example, the psychodynamic counsellor learns about the child's unconscious feelings through careful observation of the child's play. The child pushes out or projects those feelings and anxieties that are unbearable and the toys or materials used in the therapy room or the counsellor become the recipients of these projections. Similarly it can be helpful to think about dynamics in a residential care home in terms of the clients projecting their difficult feelings and the staff can become the recipients of these projections. Halton notes that in such situations, different staff members may be vulnerable to being recipients for different projected feelings. The staff's vulnerability may be related to their own past experiences of caring relationships. Moylan (1994) expands on this idea and suggests that when the emotional and physical pain in service users is overwhelming for them they may get rid of these feelings by projecting them onto staff. This has a profound effect on the staff team and they too deal with the difficult feelings by projecting them. Moylan (1994) suggests that as a result the whole organisation can become embroiled in the pain and the distressed state of mind that service users experience. This stress can be alleviated if the members of the organisation are helped to take a step back and to use their feelings to understand what is going on. By raising their consciousness staff will be able to tackle problems in an effective, appropriate way rather than resorting to avoidance or despair.

In staff consultation, transference and countertransference are very important. In a group of people, transference feelings are often very strong. Consultation sessions can be used to help to name some of the feelings experienced and to make the feeling explicit. Consultation can also provide a means of containing difficult feelings in Bion's sense and can help staff in processing the raw projected feelings of service users into a manageable form.

Schein (1987) developed a method of process consultation in order to help staff groups help themselves with difficulties that they come up against in their work. Arthur (1999) suggests that Schien's model can be helpful in offering consultation to staff groups working with people with learning disabilities and help to develop therapeutic skills. By offering an experience of solving problems within the staff group, it is expected that this will lead to a greater understanding about how to solve difficulties and allow the staff group to address such issues in the future. The consultant aims to make the feelings and emotions that exist below the surface or in the unconscious conscious and to help to make links with the processes that are present within the staff group, the client group and the organisation. The consultant comments on the process of the group, the material presented and the way in which the staff talk about their work. By helping the staff group to think about the client's internal world, and their psychosocial development through discussion of past history and previous relationships, a deeper understanding of the service users' current emotional functioning can be achieved.

CASE EXAMPLE: Consultation to Vincent's care staff

A referral was made by a group of residential staff asking for help because they were having difficulties with Vincent, one of the residents. The staff worked in a group home for five people with mild to moderate learning disabilities. Vincent was the youngest member of the household and initially appeared to be the focus of the staff's difficulties. Staff brought a number of issues related in some way to Vincent and his behaviour to the consultation meetings, including working with clients with mental health difficulties, dealing with verbal aggression, being asked repeated questions and detailed accounts of the difficult relationship between Vincent and his parents.

Over the course of the year in which the consultation took place, the home's manager left and the deputy manager started acting up as manager. During the process of talking to the staff team the consultant learned of feelings of helplessness, hopelessness, and a frequent feeling that all would be well if Vincent would move out, as he regularly threatened he would. They felt they needed to help him move on, that they did not have the skills to work with people with mental health problems.

The consultation sessions were used to help the staff to make sense of Vincent's experiences in perspective with his personal history. The staff talked about what they knew about his early experience and what they could surmise from what he told them of his relationship with his parents. The staff were able to relate these observations to the way Vincent reacted to them. We discussed how the way that Vincent related to them might indicate projections of his internal world.

The consultation sessions offered an opportunity for the staff team to explore their reactions to Vincent's behaviour. They learnt that different staff members experienced different but equally strong feelings when confronted with working with Vincent. One staff member said that when Vincent repeated the same questions she would be left feeling hopeless and deskilled, as if she had missed the point of his communication. Another found he worried about Vincent when he went out alone and did not trust that he would not get into trouble despite the evidence that he could get himself to and from college safely. He felt protective towards Vincent yet worked very hard at making sure that Vincent's independence was addressed as part of his care plan. Another staff member said that she found Vincent's verbally abusive behaviour overwhelming. She would manage this feeling by trying to ignore him and concentrate on practical tasks around the home. She said that this surprised and distressed her, as she did not experience such feelings with other residents. The staff said that it was helpful to explore their own feelings and what might be Vincent's projected feelings. They were able to identify that Vincent was a vulnerable person, that he appeared to put

Continued

himself into vulnerable situations and evoke protective feelings as a result. It was speculated that the staff's experience might mirror Vincent's early experience with his primary carers and that they may be experiencing a projection of Vincent's own feelings of hopelessness and his experience of incompetence as a result of his learning disability.

During the period of the consultation, one staff member, Kate, was off work for three weeks following an incident where Vincent had head-butted her and broken her nose in an angry outburst. On returning to work Kate explained that she had initially felt furious with Vincent and frightened to return to work, and as time had passed she had also begun to doubt her colleagues were supporting her as Vincent had been aggressive to other staff and she was left feeling abandoned and increasingly depressed. The other staff members were surprised that Vincent had attacked Kate. They described her as very gentle and caring towards the residents and perhaps the most tolerant of Vincent's difficult behaviour. Kate was able to reveal that she had felt particularly let down by the house manager who had left soon after the incident and how she thought he had not supported her need for extended leave as fully as he might have because his mind was on leaving and his new job. We explored the group processes at play. The group were losing their leader and the deputy manager was planning to 'act up' into the manager role. It was a time of transition for everyone and the consultant speculated that both staff and residents may be feeling vulnerable and uncontained. It was established that, shortly before the incident, Kate had announced she would be getting married, and would be going away after the wedding for several weeks honeymoon. We discussed the possibility of Vincent's feeling close and sexually attracted to Kate and as a result feeling rejected and angry about her future plans. Vincent's feelings may have been complicated by also losing the manager. We explored some of the Oedipal feelings that this might have evoked in Vincent with both Kate and the manager away from the house at the same time.

The consultant and the staff group aimed to differentiate when different approaches might be appropriate in helping manage or contain Vincent's difficult behaviour. It was clear that at times, when Vincent presented as withdrawn and low in mood, that staff were able to shift his mood by directing and encouraging him to participate in tasks. However, when he was repeatedly questioning or his mood was escalating towards an angry outburst, reflecting and interpretations that put his feelings into words were helpful in reducing his anxiety.

Over the period of one year, meeting on a monthly basis and using the process consultancy model, the staff group became more able to see what role their own feelings or their own position in the team played in their feelings of stress. No formal evaluation tools were used during this consultations; however, the outcome ensured that the staff them were able to identify their limitations and put pressure on the local community mental health team to offer Vincent an assessment. The staff were also able to mobilise the organisation into giving them some further training relating to working with people with learning disabilities and mental health problems.

Process consultation has three distinct phases. These are:

- Raising awareness and developing understanding of emotional lives of clients/service users.
- Thinking about emotional reactions to clients for instance, helping people to recognise transference and counter transference feelings.
- Talking about group processes and helping staff to apply some of the group processes to their group (clients and staff)

In addition, process consultation aims to help in the development of counselling skills, for instance listening, reflecting and interpreting roles rather than directing, advising and guiding. These areas are all illustrated in the consultation to Vincent's staff team.

Formal training with staff

There has been varied evidence of the impact of staff training on staff practice and consequently on changes in residents' behaviour. The majority of the literature suggests staff training has a positive effect (for example Jahr, 1998; McDonnell, 1997). However, other studies show that although feedback from training workshops is good and staff knowledge on the topic of training is increased, skills do not generalise to the workplace and there is no significant change in staff practice (Smith *et al.*, 1992).

It is generally recognised that staff caring for people with learning disabilities are often under-trained and staff training tends to be seen as a luxury rather than a necessity. Quigley *et al.* (2001) asked 116 health and social care staff working with people with learning disabilities about their knowledge of symptoms of mental health problems with the client group. They found that of the 71 per cent who supported people with a recognised mental health problem, only 47 per cent had received training in this area.

Training can be a useful means of changing attitudes in staff groups (Hastings, 1998). Through teaching new skills and giving time and space to reflect on experiences in the workplace and offering new ways of viewing difficulties, organisations can influence changes in behaviour of staff.

CASE EXAMPLE: Training package to help staff working with people with challenging behaviour

A clinical psychology service developed a comprehensive training package aimed to help both paid and unpaid care staff to work positively with people with learning disabilities and challenging needs. It was considered important to think about the emotional impact of challenging behaviour on the carers and try to address this issue from a psychodynamic perspective to help develop carers' understanding of the processes underlying difficult behaviour. One of the group exercises aims to look at projection as a means of understanding challenging behaviour. The trainers ask the participants to make a list of the reasons they think their clients might be acting in a challenging manner. The group are then asked to complete another list of feelings that they have experienced when they have been in a challenging situation. Invariably the lists are very similar and include feelings of frustration, a sense of failure, being unable to make needs or wishes understood, and feeling hopeless and helpless, powerless, angry and upset. The trainers highlight the similarity of the two lists and engage the group in a discussion. The facilitators explain that the feelings the carers are experiencing when faced with difficult behaviour are often the projected feelings of the clients. In an evaluation of this training package, staff reported that this aspect of the training gave them most insight into their clients' behaviour and generally staff found it a helpful way of thinking about their reactions to difficult behaviour and a useful basis from which to think about how best to intervene in potentially difficult situations.

CASE EXAMPLE: Bereavement and transition training for a group of staff about to embark on a major transition

A referral was made to the learning disabilities service asking for some training for staff working in a group home for five people with learning disabilities. The home was due to close and the residential service manager was concerned that the staff did not have the skills to prepare the residents adequately for the move. The learning disabilities service had a bereavement and transition training package that the residential care provider had been offered on a previous occasion, with very positive feedback. During negotiations with the residential service manager it became clear that the staff group did not yet know what would be happening to their jobs when the home closed. The service manager hoped to re-deploy all the staff within existing residential projects, but had not discussed the matter with the financial arm of the organisation, and was therefore not in a position to discuss the issue with the staff group. The consultant advised that training would not currently be effective for the staff as their own anxiety about their future would act as a block to learning the skills being offered.

Continued

As an alternative intervention the consultant agreed to support the service manager in setting up a series of two-way communication sessions with the staff group where difficult issues and feelings could be aired. Following these meetings the staff were offered the opportunity to undertake the workshop on transition and bereavement; they welcomed the opportunity and reported that the training had been helpful in motivating and guiding them to organise comprehensive transition plans for all of the residents.

SUMMARY

- Process consultation (Schein, 1987) can be an effective way of working psychodynamically with care staff and organisations.
- It is important to assess the most appropriate level at which to offer consultation. A psychodynamic approach can be helpful at different levels: in supporting staff to allow individual therapy to take place, by consulting with staff groups to help them to think about the roles that they take in the lives of people with learning disabilities, and by teaching staff groups through training courses.
- A consultation model can provide staff with deeper understanding of their clients' difficulties, and also raise their awareness of the part their own emotions and reactions play in relationships with clients and colleagues.

9

RESEARCH AND EVALUATION

Counselling can be an expensive resource compared with other treatments such as medical or behavioural approaches. Talking treatments require more time and often more resources, for example, the provision of a consistent protected environment, such as a room set aside specifically for counselling. In order to give open support for working in this way, employers or managers will usually require some evidence that it is an effective use of time and resources. This requirement is even more significant in the climate of increased division between the purchasers and the providers of services. Purchasers have to weigh up how best to spend limited budgets, whilst often remaining at a distance from the 'hands on' work. Therefore one important reason for carrying out research is to provide the evidence that one's intervention is a productive and worthwhile use of limited resources. Evidence-based practice is an integral aspect of Clinical Governance, the process by which service quality is addressed from several perspectives.

Another important reason for undertaking research is that it can enable us to learn more about which aspects of counselling are the most helpful and the most useful for particular kinds of clients and their presenting difficulties. For example, some therapists view any 'talking' treatment to be beneficial to a person in distress. They consider that it is the non-specific factors of the working alliance such as warmth, interest and empathy that are the critical aspects of talking treatment that encourage change or development (Orlinsky et al., 1994). Whilst it is no doubt true that empathic communication can be of real value, it is unlikely in itself to fully address a client's defence systems, such as projection and secondary handicap. It is essential therefore that different elements of treatment such as the making of interpretations, or challenging defences, are evaluated so that their validity can be demonstrated and argued.

A third important area of study is comparing different therapeutic approaches to get an appreciation of the relative effectiveness of different treatment modalities. This understanding gives us the possibility of using the most helpful and relevant approach for the particular client and presenting problem. For example, in the case of Mrs Clark and Louise in chapter three, a mother and daughter who appeared to be enmeshed (or in primary identification with each other), a decision had to be made about whether to provide individual counselling or family therapy, or a combination of the two. Although many factors need to be taken into account, such as client choice, practical arrangements and any current life events or stages of the family members, evidence of treatment effectiveness for their presenting difficulties has to be a major consideration.

Published outcome research into therapy with people with learning disabilities

As far as can be ascertained, there have been relatively few published research studies on counselling and psychodynamic psychotherapy with people with learning disabilities. There have been two large-scale literature reviews, specifically looking at this area, both of which have also failed to identify any substantial studies (Beail, 1995; Hurley, 1989). The outcome studies that have made it to print have almost entirely been of single case studies, or descriptions of the model with examples. Although interesting and informative about processes, these case studies cannot provide us with the opportunity to either generalise or to reliably replicate any findings. This is in marked contrast to research publications that focus on behavioural or medical interventions, where numerous large-scale studies with control groups have been published (Hurley, 1989; Nezu and Nezu, 1994). Below we consider some of the reasons why the area of counselling adults with learning disabilities has been so poorly studied. Firstly, though, we shall look in more detail at the most informative published outcome studies, where the number of participants is greater than one, therefore excluding single case studies.

The Beail Studies

Nigel Beail, a clinical psychologist working in the north of England, and his colleagues, have designed increasingly stringent and sophisticated studies (Beail and Warden, 1996, and Beail, 1998). In a paper published in 1996, Beail and Warden described how they set up measures to investigate the effectiveness of psychodynamic psychotherapy with adults with learning disabilities, and reported some of their preliminary data. In this study they described the outcome data on ten participants (nine men and one woman) who appeared to fall into the mild to moderate learning disabilities range. The participants undertook once weekly psychodynamic psychotherapy from five to forty-eight sessions with a mean of eighteen sessions. The measures were the Symptom Checklist (Derogatis, 1975) and the Rosenburg Self Esteem Scale (Rosenburg, 1965), presented in an interview format by psychology assistants at intervals of eight sessions. Both measures are checklists describing various symptoms or thoughts in which the participant is required to state whether they have experienced that symptom in the last week or month. The authors note that both questionnaires needed to be adapted to be presented in interview format, rather than being filled in by the participants themselves. In their sample, there was a significant rise in the self-esteem measures and decrease in the symptom measures after treatment. They have noted that the sample size was small, and that there was no control group. The value of a control group is that, through assessing people who are matched with the 'treatment group', who do not undergo treatment, significant developments in the treatment group can be more reliably attributed to the treatment, rather than other factors. Beail and Warden (1996) argue that randomised control trials are not always feasible, it may not be possible to find matched controls, and may not always be preferable, so they argue instead for naturalistic studies of normal clinical practice.

In 1998, Beail published the results of another outcome study, apparently unrelated to the 1996 study. This concerned the impact of psychodynamic psychotherapy on 25 men with learning disabilities and behavioural problems. The participants were recruited from a forensic service, and because aggressive behaviour was a key symptom, they were able to measure an observable behaviour before and after short-term psychodynamic psychotherapy. They found a significant reduction in aggressive behaviour at the end of the treatment, and impressively, at a six month follow-up.

The Tavistock Study

In 1996, Bichard, Sinason and Usiskin published the results of a three-year study that examined changes in the cognitive and emotional development of eight adults with learning disabilities who underwent long-term psychoanalytic psychotherapy. This was a rigorously designed and controlled research study, however its presence is easily overlooked owing to its placement in an American newsletter. The treatment group adults were treated either in individual therapy or in a group, but all by the same psychotherapist for at least three years. The matched control group were drawn from adults on the waiting list, who were seen for reviews and assessments at yearly intervals. The study used a range of outcome measures, completed at yearly intervals, designed to measure different symptom domains (cognitive and emotional) as well as different perspectives (the clients, the therapist and that of a close significant person).

Kazdin (1994) suggests the use of multiple measures such as these are more effective than single measures in identifying changes when looking at outcome. This study employed a variety of measures. The published study reports on the findings of the changes in the 'Draw a Person' (DAP) test. The DAP test is a *projective test*. Projective tests (although projective assessments is a more accurate term as the work 'test' implies correct or incorrect responses exist), rely on the phenomena that we tend to project aspects of ourselves, our inner worlds, into ambiguous stimuli. Bichard *et al.* (1996) argue that developments in human figure drawings can reflect changes in thinking. This view is somewhat supported by the research completed by Karen Machover who looked at several hundred human figure drawings repeated at intervals of several years. She discovered that human figure drawings remain as consistent as an individual's signature. Therefore development and change in human figure drawings is significant, and it has been argued that it reflects some form of internal development (Machover, 1949).

Bichard *et al.* (1996) found that in seven out of the eight treatment participants, their 'draw a person' results had improved, that is, their drawings had become more detailed, developed or sophisticated as measured on a standardised scale (the Goodenough-Harris scale, 1963). This finding contrasted significantly with the control group, where only one client demonstrated an improvement in their draw-a-person scores. In addition the scores continued to improve at each of the yearly assessments during the treatment period. Bichard *et al.* also note that the results from the interviews with carers demonstrate that in the majority of the treatment cases, the carers felt that the clients' symptoms had improved or disappeared, whereas for the control group, the majority of the carers considered the clients' symptoms to have either worsened or stayed the same.

Difficulties in outcome research in learning disabilities

There are relatively few systematic studies that look at the impact of psychotherapeutic approaches with people with learning disabilities. There is, however, a preponderance of research studies that report on behavioural approaches and their evaluation. Arthur (1999) notes that considerable attention is paid to the description and assessment of three main areas in working with people with learning disabilities, these are: cognitive functioning, behaviour modification and service evaluation. He notes how the inner worlds and emotional lives of people with learning disabilities are much neglected in research. Several authors have speculated as to what factors might have contributed to the apparent lack of research interest (Bailey *et al.*, 1986; Hatton *et al.*, 1999). Possible reasons that have been put forward include:

- a general lack of knowledge about the emotional world of people with learning disabilities, and how this is reflected in their behaviour;

- a pervasive belief that feelings are not relevant in understanding people with learning disabilities;
- until the recent policy of deinstitutionalisation, people with learning disabilities have been relatively invisible, segregated in large hospitals;
- the existence of negative stereotypes;
- the lack of prestige in working in learning disabilities, and associated with this there is a difficulty in getting financial support and grants;
- the client group might be perceived as uninteresting because of their associated cognitive and adaptive skills;
- the difficulty in utilising standardised surveys and interviews;
- the difficulty in getting informed consent, and therefore ethical agreement; and
- the difficulty in finding appropriate control groups.

Although a long and somewhat disheartening list, there are potential ways to overcome the majority of these difficulties, which shall be explored later. Firstly some broader methodological issues that can interfere with the process of planning outcome studies with people with learning disabilities will be considered.

Verbal ability

Most outcome studies require some degree of verbal ability, both receptive and expressive in order to take part in interviews or to complete forms. This has the potential to exclude people who have limited verbal skills from research projects. Only including verbal or literate clients makes it questionable to generalise from research findings across the full client group. People with learning disabilities who have good verbal skills may not necessarily be representative of the whole client group.

Treatment equity

Psychodynamic therapists work from a foundation of psychodynamic and psychoanalytic theory and techniques, of which there are a wide range (Freudian based, Kleinian based, Jungian, Lacanian, and so on). Most contemporary psychoanalytically-orientated therapists tend to have derived their treatments from a range of theoretical bases, which although clinically appropriate for the clients, make comparisons between research studies very difficult. Counselling and therapy for people with learning disabilities is a relatively recent development and at this point in time there is no agreed consensus about which particular approaches are the most helpful.

There is also the issue of how theories are put into practice; there are bound to be individual differences in terms of style and delivery of therapy. There are a range of post qualification trainings, and as yet there is no formal body organising and co-ordinating this specialism in psychology or counselling, although more recently a formal body for the psychotherapy of learning disabilities (as a branch of the British Association of Psychotherapy) has been established. Arthur (1999) has commented that differences in approach are not just in training – personality also plays a role. He describes this as 'unique personality and cognitive epistemological styles'. He also connects personal attributes with choices in research methodology. These ideas are equally applicable to clinicians working across a range of disciplines with people with learning disabilities.

Number of participants

Although counselling adults with learning disabilities is becoming a more mainstream treatment area, counsellors who specifically specialise in work with adults with learning disabilities are still in the minority. This means that each counsellor may only have a few cases on which to base any study or investigation. Counsellors often work in isolation so only have their own case load, or at the most the case load from a small team, from which to draw participants. The combination of small case loads and longer term treatment inevitably lead to small sample sizes, which has the obvious effect of limiting the ability to generalise from the results. One solution would be for individuals or departments to link up to create a larger sample, though this solution has its own difficulties, such as ensuring equitable treatments are provided in each service.

Reliance on retrospective methods

The majority of outcome studies have some interview or rating component, which normally require either the client, the therapist or significant others to make judgements about past events. There is some evidence that people with learning disabilities may be susceptible to responding in certain ways such as acquiescence (Chapman and Oakes, 1995) and in a socially acceptable way (Barker *et al.*, 1995). There is also the issue of organic (as well as emotional) impairment to memory which may interfere with a person's ability to accurately recall events and inner states.

Measurement tools and standardisation

There are a limited number of assessments that have been standardised with people with learning disabilities. However, these tend to explore consequences of the person's disability rather than personality or psychological symptoms, which may of course, be unrelated or indirectly related, to the disability. Assessment tools that explore psychological and personality factors tend to be lengthy and require a high level of verbal and or reading skills. Adapting these is possible, but this may interfere with any standardisation data, making interpretation of the results and comparisons between studies difficult.

As already mentioned, there have been suggestions that people with learning disabilities are prone to acquiescent response biases when using questionnaire and analogue scales. Although this needs to be considered in designing an outcome study, Dagnan and Ruddick (1995) explored the reliability and validity of these methods with a group of mild to moderately learning disabled adults. They found that relatively sophisticated question formats could be used with this client group, and a good degree of reliability could be achieved. They did find, however, that the people with better receptive language skills managed the questionnaire format better than those with a lower ability. This tendency was not apparent for the pictorial analogue scale.

Consent

Consent in providing treatment to people with learning disabilities is a contentious issue, before research has even been considered. The issues around consent to therapy include the following difficulties and questions:

- When clients are escorted by carers to sessions, there is a question as to whether the problem is with the client or the wider system.
- Has the client been presented with treatment options and their possible impacts?
- Is he or she cognitively able to make an informed choice?

Consent to psychological research presents additional difficulties. Arscott *et al.* (1998) investigated this issue and found that although their participants (40 people with a range of mild to severe learning disabilities) appeared to understand what the study was about, they had much less of an understanding regarding the risks and benefits of the research, or of their right to refuse to participate or indeed to withdraw at any stage. This finding is in common with research that indicates that people with learning disabilities have a tendency to please others, in order to minimise negative projections (Chapman and Oakes, 1995). Arscott *et al.* (1998) conclude that researchers must assess the ability of participants to consent to studies, prior to any data collection.

Recommendations for research

Although there are a number of difficulties and considerations in undertaking research, these are not insurmountable. We need not become overwhelmed and discouraged, as it is important that some effort is made to undertake outcome research so that we can gain a greater understanding about the effectiveness of various forms of treatments. It is also important to tease out which aspects of treatments are significant in the work with people with learning disabilities. It is better to establish a research study with some clearly specified compromises, (for example because of resources or circumstances) than to give up altogether in the face of problems. We will then generate some data with which we can develop new understandings, ideas and hypotheses for further exploration. For example, rich and invaluable data can be generated from small qualitative studies such as those by Bichard *et al.* (1996) and Beail (1998), that can guide practice or future research.

Very few practitioners are in the position where they have the resources to produce large-scale randomised control trial outcome studies. Clinical audit, the process of measuring the effectiveness of one's own approaches against a preset standard, can provide helpful feedback on local treatment outcomes (see Davenhill, 1998), as can small-scale quality assurance methods such as feedback forms and questionnaires. It is also unlikely that funding will be readily available for larger or more sophisticated studies until more conclusive and consistent results have been published. This may require creative uses of resources such as departments linking up to increase participant numbers, as is happening in a nation-wide study based at St George's Medical School (Hollins, 2001, personal communication).

Kazdin (1994) has identified that outcome studies are most effective if they make measurements across several domains, such as cognitive, emotional and behavioural. Studies that incorporate measures which can access a client's functioning in different domains are likely to be more sensitive. In addition, drawing from a number of sources will increase the sensitivity (and validity) of measures, so, for example, collecting measures from the client themselves, the counsellor and a significant other such as a key-worker or family member is a sensible route. It may be possible to construct a robust evaluation with a range of measures from different sources as is the case in the outcome of therapy studies published to date (Beail and Warden, 1996; Beail, 1998; Bichard et al., 1996).

Studies which incorporate larger client numbers are not necessarily the only way forward in outcome evaluation. Single case designs can yield very rich data, especially when clear base-lines have been taken and a degree of methodological rigour is utilised. Jill Hodges suggests that the single case design may have an important role in 'building bridges' between psycho-dynamic approaches and other treatment types (Hodges, 1999), and has been successfully used to systematically examine out-comes for a child with learning disabilities and autism (Reid, 1997). Keeping detailed records of sessions and of discussions in supervision can provide large amounts of data for examina-tion, as can video recordings or tapes of sessions. Another im-portant level of understanding that cannot be made without reference to the counsellor's experience is by incorporating understandings made through transference and countertransference communications.

The single case design is frequently used in evaluating behavioural techniques, and we could consider 'borrowing' other research strategies from different fields of study. Family therapists often rely on detailed qualitative analysis of transcripts of sessions or interviews to produce helpful information about their treatments, and studies of people with learning disabilities are starting to use qualitative methods more readily (for example Mattison and Pistrang, 2000). Child development research could offer many strategies for people who have no or little language. Valuable data about infants' internal worlds, social, perceptual and cognitive development have been gathered by studying minute interactions, sometimes through analysing video recordings frame by frame.

Other methods that are used in child research can be adapted for people with learning disabilities. Understandings about a person's perception of themselves can be taken over time using repertory grid techniques (Ryle, 1975) at regular intervals. This is a research method whereby a person is asked to place themselves and significant others on a range of different concepts (for example, happy, sad, lonely, curious and so on), and any shifts in perceptions of self and others over time can reflect internal developments. Pictures and diagrams can be used to represent the concepts, allowing for language difficulties. This method has been successfully employed by Skene (1991) in assessing the outcome of group psychotherapy for adults with learning disabilities. Ryle (1975) provides a helpful introduction to repertory grid techniques.

There are a range of techniques and strategies that can be used in very fruitful studies of the utility of counselling treatments. It may be that the randomised control study has a place in learning disabilities research, but it may also be that the field needs to 'catch up' with other mainstream treatment areas, by the creative use of well-established research strategies.

SUMMARY

- In comparison with other groups (such as mental health treatment) or treatments of this population with other methods (such as behavioural), outcome in this area is very under-researched.

- Outcome research in counselling people with learning disabilities is unpopular for a range of reasons, such as consent issues being more ambiguous, and the need for verbal ability/cognitive skills to respond to standardised tools.
- The design of large-scale randomised treatment groups with adequate controls have proved to be very problematic, and may only be one way forward.
- It may be more fruitful to draw on successful methodologies from other areas such as the single case design, qualitative methods and careful analysis of process records. Whilst many research designs may feel less rigorous compared with the impressive large-scale, randomised controlled studies, valuable and important information can be ignored or lost without recourse to a range of different methodologies.

REFERENCES

Alvarez, A. (1989) 'Development Towards the Latency Period: Splitting and the need to forget in borderline children', *Journal of Child Psychotherapy* 15(2), 71–83.

Alvarez, A. (1992) *Live Company* (London: Routledge).

Alvarez, A. and Reid, S. (1999) *Autism and Personality* (London: Routledge).

Andrews, J. (1996) 'Identifying and Providing for the Mentally Disabled in Early Modern London', in D. Wright and A. Digby (eds) *From Idiocy to Mental Deficiency: Historical Perspectives on People with Learning Disabilities* (London: Routledge).

Arscott, K., Dagnan, D. and Stenfert-Kroese, B. (1998) 'Consent to Psychological Research by People with an Intellectual Disability', *Journal of Applied Research in Intellectual Disabilities* Vol. 11, No. 1, 77–83.

Arthur, A.R. (1999) 'Using Staff Consultation to Facilitate the Emotional Development of Adults with Learning Disabilities', *Journal of Learning Disabilities* 27, 93–8.

Atkinson, D., Jackson, M. and Walmsley, J. (1997) *Forgotten Lives: Exploring the history of learning disabilities* (BILD publications).

Atkinson, N. and Crawford, M. (1995) *All in the Family: Siblings and Disability* (London: NCH Action for Children).

Aveline, M. and Dryden, W. (1988) (eds) *Group Therapy in Britain* (Open University Press).

Bailey, R., Matthews, S. and Leckie, L. (1986) 'Feeling the Way Ahead in Mental Handicap', *Mental Handicap* 14, 65–7.

Barker, C., Pistrang, N. and Elliott, R. (1995) *Research Methods in Clinical and Counselling Psychology* (Chichester: Wiley).

Barnes, B., Ernst, S. and Hyde, K. (1999) *An Introduction to Group Work* (Basingstoke: Palgrave Macmillan).

Barnes, C. (1994) *Disabled People in Britain and Discrimination; A case for anti-discrimination legislation* (London: Hurst and Company in association with BCODP).

Bateman, A. and Holmes, J. (1995) *Introduction to Psychoanalysis: Contemporary Theory and Practice* (London: Routledge).

Beail, N. (1995) 'Outcome of Psychoanalysis, Psychoanalytic and Psychodynamic Psychotherapy with People with Intellectual Disabilities: a review', *Changes* 13, 186–91.

Beail, N. (1998) 'Psychoanalytic Psychotherapy with Men with Intellectual Disabilities: A preliminary outcome study', *British Journal of Medical Psychology* 71, 1–11.

Beail, N. and Warden, S. (1996) 'Evaluation of a Psychodynamic Psychotherapy Service for Adults with Intellectual Disabilities: rationale, design and preliminary outcome data', *Journal of Applied Research in Intellectual Disabilities* 9(3), 223–8.

Bender, M. (1993) 'The Unoffered Chair: the history of therapeutic disdain towards people with learning disabilities', *Clinical Psychology Forum* 54, 7–12.

Bender, M. Tombs, D. Hodges, S. Morris, R. and Finnis, S. (1992) 'How Should we Measure the Effect of Groupwork with Adults with Learning Difficulties: i Outcome Variables', *Clinical Psychology Forum* 43, 2–6.

Bichard, S.H. Sinason, V. and Usiskin, J. (1996) 'Measuring Change in Mentally Retarded Clients in Long Term Psychoanalytic Psychotherapy – 1 The Draw-a-Person Test', *NADD Newsletter* 13(5), 6–11.

Bick, E. (1964) 'Notes on Infant Observation in Psychoanalytic Training', *International Journal of Psychoanalysis* 45, 558–66.

Bick, E. (1968) 'The Experience of the Skin in Early Object Relationships', *International Journal of Psychoanalysis* 49, 484–6.

Bick, E. (1986) 'Further Considerations of the Function of the Skin in Early Object Relations', *British Journal of Psychotherapy* 2(4), 292–9.

Bicknell, J. (1983) 'The Psychopathology of Handicap', *British Journal of Medical Psychology* 56(2), 167–78.

Bion, W. (1959) 'Attacks on Linking', *International Journal of Psychoanalysis* 40, 308–15.

Bion, W.R. (1961) *Experiences in Groups and Other Papers* (London: Routledge).

Bion, W.R. (1962a) *Learning From Experience* (London: Heinemann).

Bion, W.R. (1962b) 'The Theory of Thinking', *International Journal of Psychoanalysis* 43, 4–5.

Bion, W.R. (1967) *Second Thoughts* (reprinted 1984) (London: Karnac).

Booth, T. and Booth, W. (1994) *Parenting under pressure* (Buckingham: Open University Press).

Boss, P. (1991) 'Ambiguous Loss', in F. Walsh and M. McGoldrick (eds) *Living Beyond Loss: Death in the family* (London: W.W. Norton).

Bower, M. (1995) 'Psychodynamic Family Therapy with Parents and Under-five's', in J. Trowell and M. Bower (eds) *The Emotional Needs of Young Children and Their Families: Using Psychoanalytic Ideas in the Community* (London: Routledge).

Bowlby, J. (1988) *A Secure Base: Clinical Applications of Attachment Theory* (London: Routledge).

Boyce, G.C. and Barnett, W.S. (1993) 'Siblings of Persons with Mental Retardation: historical perspectives and recent findings', in Z. Stoneman and P. Waldman-Berman (eds) *The Effects of Mental Retardation, Disability and Illness on Sibling Relationships: Research Issues and Challenges* (Baltimore: Paul H. Brookes Publishing Co.).

Brandon, D. (ed) (1989) *Mutual Respect: Therapeutic Approaches to People who have Learning Difficulties* (Surbiton, Surrey: Good Impressions).

Bratt, A. and Johnston, R. (1988) 'Changes in Lifestyle for Young Adults with Profound Handicaps Following Discharge from Hospital Care to "Second Generation" Housing Project', *Mental Handicap Research* 1, 49–74.

Brelstaff, K. (1984) 'Reactions to Death: can the mentally handicapped grieve: The experience of some who did', *Teaching and Training* 22, 1–17.

Brown, D. and Pedder, J. (1979) Introduction to Psychotherapy (London: Routledge).

Brown, H. (1996) 'Ordinary Women: Issues for Women with Learning Disabilities: A keynote review', *British Journal of Learning Disabilities* 24(2), 47–51.

Brown, H. (1999) *Living in Fear* (London: Mencap Publications).

Brown, H. and Craft, A. (eds) (1989) *Thinking the Unthinkable: Sexual Abuse and People with Learning Disabilities* (London: Family Planning Association).

Brown, H., Stein, J. and Turk, V. (1995) 'The Sexual Abuse of Adults with Learning Disabilities, a second incidence survey', *Mental Handicap Research* 8, 3–23.

Buchanan, A. and Oliver, J.E. (1977) 'Abuse and Neglect as a Cause of Mental Retardation', *British Journal of Psychiatry* 131, 458–67.

Burke, P. and Montgomery, S. (2000) 'Siblings of Children with Disabilities: a pilot study', *Journal of Learning Disabilities* 4(3), 227–36.

Burns, J. (2000) 'Gender Identity and Women with Learning Disabilities: the third sex,' *Clinical Psychology Forum* 137, 11–15 March.

Caine, A., Hatton, C. and Emerson, E. (1998) 'Service Provision', in E. Emerson, C. Hatton, J. Bromley and A. Caine (eds) *Clinical Psychology and People with Intellectual Disabilities* (Chichester: J. Wiley and Sons).

Cambridge, P. (1997b) 'How far to gay? The politics of HIV in learning disabilities', *Disability and Society* 12, 427–53.

Carr, J. (1988) 'Six Weeks to Twenty-one Years Old: A longitudinal study of children with Down's syndrome and their families', *Journal of Child Psychology and Psychiatry* 29, 4, 407–31.

Carter, E.A. and McGoldrick, M. (1980) *The Family Life Cycle: A Framework for Family Therapy* (London and New York: Gardner Press).

Chapman, K. and Oakes, P. (1995) 'Asking People with Learning Disabilities their Views on Direct Psychological Interventions,' *Clinical Psychology Forum* 81, 28–33.

Clark, P. (1933) *The Nature and Treatment of Amentia* (New York: Bailliere).

Clegg, J. (1996) 'Psychotherapy in Learning Disabilities', *British Journal of Clinical Psychology* 35, 321–2.

Coffman, T.L. and Harris, M.C. (1980) 'Transition Shock and Adjustments in Mentally Retarded Persons', *Mental Retardation* 18, 3–7.

Conboy-Hill, S. and Waitman, A. (eds) (1992) *Psychotherapy and Mental Handicap* (London: Sage).

Corbett, A., Cottis, T. and Morris, S. (1996) *Witnessing, Nurturing and Protesting: Therapeutic responses to sexual abuse of people with learning disabilities* (London: David Fulton Publishers).

Craft, A. (1987) *Mental Handicap and Sexuality: Issues and Perspectives* (Tunbridge Wells: Costello).

Craft, A. (ed) (1994) *Practice Issues in Sexuality and Mental Handicap* (London: Routledge).

Craft, A. and Brown, H. (1994) 'Personal Relationships and Sexuality: the staff role', in A. Craft (ed) *Practice Issues in Sexuality and Learning Disabilities* (London. Routledge).

Craft, A. and Craft, M. (1979) *Handicapped Married Couples* (London: Routledge and Kegan Paul).

Craft, M., Bicknall, J. and Hollins, S. (1985) *Mental Handicap: A Multi-disciplinary Approach* (New York: Balliere Tindall).

Dagnan, D. and Ruddick, L. (1995) 'The Use of Analogue Scales and Personal Questionnaires for Interviewing People with Learning Disabilities', *Clinical Psychology Forum 79*, 21–3.

Dale, N. (1995) *Working With Families of Children With Special Needs* (London: Routledge).

Davenhill, R. (1998) *Rethinking Clinical Audit: The case of psychotherapy services in the NHS* [London: Routledge].

Derogatis, L.R. (1975) *Brief Symptom Inventory* (Balitmore: Clinical Psychometric Research).

De Groef, J. (1999) 'Mental Handicaps: A Dark Continent', in J. De Groef and E. Heinemann (eds) *Psychoanalysis and Mental Handicap* (London: Routledge).

Department of Health (1971) *Better Services for the Mentally Handicapped* (London: HMSO).

Department of Health (1990) *NHS and Community Care Act* (London: HMSO).

Department of Health (1997) *Who Decides? Making Decisions on Behalf of Incapacitated Adults* (London: HMSO).

Department of Health (1999) *Effective Care Co-ordination in Mental Health Services: Modernising the Care Programme Approach* (NSF).

Department of Health (1999) *Still Building Bridges* (London: HMSO).

Department of Health (2000) *The Children Act Report* (London: HMSO).

Department of Health (2001) *Planning for Health and Social Care* (London: HMSO).

Dorney, M. (1999) 'Group Work with Women with Learning Disabilities', *British Journal of Learning Disabilities 27*, 132–6.

Dowdney, L. and Skuse, D. (1993) 'Parenting Provided by Adults with Mental Retardation', *Journal of Child Psychology and Psychiatry 34*, 25–37.

Dunn, J. and Kendrick, C. (1982) *Siblings: Love Envy and Understanding* (London: Grant McIntyre).

Dyer, S. and Quinn, L. (1998) 'Predictors of Job Satisfaction and Burnout among the Direct Care Staff of a Community Learning Disabilities Service,' *Journal of Applied Research in Intellectual Disabilities 11*(4), 320–32.

Education Act (1971) London: HMSO.

Emerson, E. (2001) *Challenging Behaviour: Analysis and Intervention in People with Intellectual Disabilities* (2nd edn) (Cambridge: Cambridge University Press).

Emerson, E., Kiernan, C., Alborez, A., Reeves, D. and Mason, H. (2001) 'Challenging Behaviours: a total population study', *Research in Developmental Disabilities* (in press).

Emerson, E., Hatton, C., Felce, D. and Murphy, G. (2001) *Learning Disabilities: The fundamental facts* (London: The Mental Health Foundation).

Emerson, E. and Hatton, C. (1994) *Moving Out: The Impact of Relocation from Hospital to Community on Quality of Life for People with Learning Disabilities* (London: HMSO).

Emmanuel, L. (1997) 'Facing the Damage Together: some reflections arising from the treatment in psychotherapy of a severely mentally handicapped child', *Journal of Child Psychotherapy* 23(2), 279–302.

Emmanuel, R. (1984) 'Primary Disappointment', *Journal of Child Psychotherapy* 10(1), 71–87.

Evans, A. and Midence, K. (1999) 'Is There a Role for Family Therapy in Adults with Learning Disabilities?' *Clinical Psychology Forum* 129, 30–3.

Evans, J., Jones, J. and Mansell, I. (2001) 'Supporting Siblings: evaluation of support groups for brothers and sisters of children with learning disabilities and challenging behaviour', *Journal of Learning Disabilities* 5(1), 69–78.

Felce, D., Lowe, K. and Beswick, J. (1993) 'Staff Turnover in Ordinary Housing Services for People with Severe or Profound Mental Handicaps', *Journal of Intellectual Disability Research* 37, 143–52.

Felce, D., Lunt, B. and Kushlick, A. (1980) 'Evaluation of Alternative Residential Facilities for the Severely Mentally' handicapped in Wessex: family contact, Advances in *Behaviour, Research and Therapy* 3, 19–23.

Ferenczi, Sandor (1929) 'The Unwelcome Child and his Death Instinct', in M. Balint (1955) *Sandor Ferenczi: Final Contributions to the Problems and Methods of Psychoanalysis* (London: Hogarth Press).

Flynn, M. (1989) *Independent Living for Adults with Mental Handicap: a place of my own* (London: Cassell).

Foulkes, S.H. (1948) *Introduction to Group Analytic Psychotherapy* (London: Maresfield Reprints).

Foulkes, S.H. (1964) *Therapeutic Group Analysis* (London: Allen and Unwin).

Frankish, P. (1992) 'A Psychodynamic Approach to Emotional Difficulties within a Social Framework', *Journal of Intellectual Disability Research* 36, 295–305.

Fraser, W. and Nolan, M. (1995) 'Psychiatric Disorders in Mental Retardation', in N. Bouras (ed) *Mental Health in Mental Retardation: Recent advances and practices* (Cambridge: Cambridge University Press).

Freud, S. (1904) 'Loewenfeld, 'Freud's Psycho-analytic', in James Strachey (ed) *The Standard Edition of the complete works of Sigmund Freud*, 24 vols (London: Hogarth Press), 953–73 (known as Standard Edition.), SE 7, 249–54.

Freud, S. (1905) 'Fragment of an Analysis of a Case of Hysteria', *Standard Edition* 7 pp 3–122.

Freud, S. (1910) 'The Future Prospects of Psychoanalysis', *Standard Edition* 11 (London: Hogarth Press).

Freud, S. (1912) 'Recommendations to Physicians Practising Psycho-analysis', *Standard Edition* 12 (London: Hogarth Press).

Freud, S. (1914) 'On Narcissism: an introduction', in James Strachey (ed) *Standard Edition* Vol 14, 67–102.

Freud, S. (1918) 'From the History of an Infantile Neurosis', *Standard Edition* 17 pp 3–123.

Frith, H. and Rapley, M. (1990) *From Acquaintance to Friendship: issues for people with learning disabilities* (Clevedon: BIMH Publications).

Garcia, E.E. and De Haven, E.D. (1974) 'Use of Operant Techniques in the Establishment and Generalization of Language: a review and analysis', *American Journal of Mental Deficiency* 79, 169–78.

Gath, A. (1974) 'Siblings' Reactions to Mental Handicap: a comparison of brothers and sisters of mongol children', *Journal of Child Psychology and Psychiatry* 15, 187–98.

Gath, A. (1977) 'The Impact of an Abnormal Child upon the Parents', *British Journal of Psychiatry* 13, 405–10.

Gath, A. and Gumley, D. (1987) 'Retarded Children and their Siblings', *Journal of Child Psychology and Psychiatry* 28(5), 715–30.

Gavestock, S. and McGauley, G. (1994) 'Connecting confusions with painful realities: Group analytic psychotherapy with adults with learning disabilities', *Psychoanalytic Psychotherapy* 8(2), 153–67.

Glasser, M., Kolvin, I., Campbell, D. and Glasser, A. (2001) 'Cycle of Child Sexual abuse: links between being a victim and becoming a perpetrator', *British Journal of Psychiatry* 179, 482–94.

Goble, C. (1999) ' "Like the Secret Services Isn't It": people with learning difficulties' perceptions of staff and services: Mystification and disempowerment', *Disability and Society* 14(4), 449–61.

Goldberg, D., Magrill, L., Hale, J., Damaskinidou, K., Paul, J. and Tham, S. (1995) 'Protection and Loss: working with learning disabled adults and their families', *Journal of Family Therapy* 17, 263–80.

Goldberg, D. and Huxley, P. (1980) *Mental Illness in the Community* (London: Mental Health Foundation).

Grant, G. (1986) 'Older Carers, inter-dependence and Care of Mentally Handicapped Adults', *Ageing and Society* 6, 333–51.

Griffiths, G. (2001) *Making it Work: Inspection of welfare to work for disabled people* (London: Department of Health).

Gunn, M. (1994) 'Competency and Consent: the importance of decision making', in A. Craft (ed) *Sexuality and Learning Disabilities* (London: Routledge).

Halton, W. (1994) 'Some Unconscious Aspects of Organisational Life: contributions from psychoanalysis', in A. Obholzer and V. Zagier-Roberts (eds) *The Unconscious at Work: Individual and organisational stress in the human services* (London and New York: Routledge).

Harries, D. (1991) *Services for People with Learning Disabilities and Sensory Impairments* (London: Change).

Harris, D. (1963) *Goodenough-Harris Drawing Test* (New York: Harcourt Brace).

Hartland-Rowe, L. (2001) 'An Exploration of Severe Learning Disabilities in Adults and the Study of Early Interaction', *Infant Observation* 4(3), 42–62.

Hastings, R. (1998) 'Learning Disability Care Staff's Emotional Reactions to Aggressive Challenging Behaviours: development of a measurement tool,' *British Journal of Clinical Psychology* 37(4), 441–9.

Hatton, C., Hastings, R., and Vetere, A. (1999) 'A Case for Inclusion?' *The Psychologist* 12(5), 231–3.

Hatton, C., Brown, R., Caine, A. and Emerson, E. (1995) 'Stressors, Coping Strategies and Stress-related Outcomes among Direct Care Staff in Staffed Houses for People with Learning Disabilities', *Mental Handicap Research* 8(4), 252–71.

Hatton, C. and Emerson, E. (1993) 'Organisational Predictors of Staff Stress, Satisfaction and Intended Turnover in a Service for People with Multiple Disabilities', *Mental Retardation* 31(6), 388–95.

Heimann, P. (1950) 'On Countertransference', *International Journal of Psychoanalysis* 31, 81–4.

Hernandez, I. (2000) Paper Presented at the Tavistock Clinic Learning Disabilities Service Conference, March, 2000.

Hernandez, I., Hodges, S.R., Miller, L. and Simpson, D. (2000) 'A Psychotherapy Service for Children and Adults with a Learning Disability', *British Journal of Learning Disabilities* 28, 120–4.

Hinshelwood, R.D. (1991) *Clinical Klein* (London: Free Association).

Hodges, J. (1999) 'Research in Child and Adolescent Psychotherapy: an overview', in M. Lanyado and A. Horne *The Handbook of Child and Adolescent Psychotherapy* (London: Routledge).

Hollins, S. and Evered, C. (1990) 'Group Process and Content: the challenge of mental handicap', *Group Analysis* 23, 55–67.

Hollins, S. (1992) 'Group Analytic Therapy for People with a Mental Handicap', in A. Waitman and S. Conboy Hill (eds) *Psychotherapy and Mental Handicap* (London: Sage).

Hollins, S. and Esterhuyzen, A. (1997) 'Bereavement and Grief in Adults with Learning Disabilities', *British Journal of Psychiatry* 170, 497–501.

Hollins, S. and Sireling, L. (1991) *Working Together Through Loss With People Who Have a Learning Disability* (Windsor: NFER–Nelson).

Hollins, S. and Sinason V. (2000) 'Psychotherapy, Learning Disabilities and Trauma: new perspectives', *British Journal of Psychiatry* 176, 37–41.

Hurley, A.D. (1989) 'Individual Psychotherapy with Mentally Retarded Individuals: a review and call for research', *Research in Developmental Disabilities* 10, 261–75.

Iverson, J.C. and Fox, R.A. (1989) 'Prevalence of Psychopathology Among Mentally Retarded Adults', *Research in Developmental Disabilities* 10, 77–83.

Jackson, M. (1996) 'Institutional Provision for the Feeble Minded in Edwardian England: Sandlebridge and the scientific morality of permanent care', in D. Wright and A. Digby (eds) *From Idiocy to Mental Deficiency: Historical Perspectives on People with Learning Disabilities* (London: Routledge).

Jahoda, A., Cattermole, M. and Markova, I. (1990) 'Moving out: an opportunity for friendship and broadening social horizons?' *Journal of Mental Deficiency Research* 34(2), 127–41.

Jahr, E. (1998) 'Current Issues in Staff Training', *Research in Developmental Disabilities* 19(1), 73–87.

Jobling, A., Moni, K.B. and Nolan, A. (2000) 'Understanding Friendship: young adults with Down's syndrome exploring friendship', *Journal of Intellectual and Developmental Disability* 25(3), 235–45.

Jones, A. (1996) 'Group Psychotherapy with People with Learning Disabilities', *British Journal of Learning Disabilities* 24, 65–9.

Jung, C.G. (1946) *Psychological Types* (London: Routledge and Kegan Paul).

Kahr, B. (1997) 'Setting up the Treatment: first steps in psychotherapy with handicapped people', Proceedings of Conference: Psychodynamic Approaches to Learning Disability APILD, Sheffield, March.

Kavanagh, S.M. and Opit, L.J. (1999) *Transition between Children's and Adult Services for Young People with Disabilities* (London: King's Fund Project/Council for Disabled Children).

Kazdin, A.E. (1994) 'Psychotherapy for Children and Adolescents', in A.E. Bergin and S.L. Garfield (eds) *Handbook of Psychotherapy and Behaviour Change* (New York: Wiley).

Kerr, A.M. (1998) *The NHS for all? People with Learning Disabilities and Health Care* (London: Mencap).

Kim, S., Larson, S.A. and Lakin, K.C. (2001) Behavioural Outcomes of deinstitutionalisation for People with Intellectual Disabilities: a review of US studies conducted between 1980 and 1999, *Journal of Intellectual and Developmental Disabilities Special Issue: Part II Community Living and People with Intellectual Disabilites* 29(1), 35–50.

Klein, M. (1928) 'Early Stages of the Oedipus Conflict', *International Journal of Psychoanalysis* 9, 167–80.

Klein, M. (1923) 'Infant Analysis', *International Journal of Psychoanalysis* 7, 31–63.

Klein, M. (1926) 'The Psychological Principles of Early Analysis', *International Journal of Psychoanalysis* 8, 25–37.

Klein, M. (1931) 'A Contribution to the Theory of Intellectual Inhibition', in *Journal of Psychoanalysis* 12, 206–18.

Klein, M. (1932) *The Psychoanalysis of Children* (London: Hogarth Press).

Klein, M. (1952) 'Some Theoretical Conclusions Regarding the Emotional Life of the Infant', in Klein (1975) *Envy and Gratitude and other works:*

The writings of Melanie Klein, Vol. 3 (Hogarth and Institute of Psycho-analysis), 61–94.

Kloeppel, D.A. and Hollins, S. (1989) 'Double Handicap: Mental Retardation and Death in the Family', *Death Studies* 13, 31–8.

Knox, M. and Hickson, F. (2001) 'The Meaning of Close Friendship: the views of four people with intellectual disabilities', *Journal of Applied Research in Intellectual Disabilities* 14, 276–91.

Korff-Sausse, S. (1999) 'A Psychoanalytic Approach to Mental Handicap', in J. De Groef and E. Heinemann (eds) *Psychoanalysis and Mental Handicap* (London: Routledge).

Landesman-Dwyer, S. and Berkson, G. (1984) 'Friendships and Social Behaviour', in J. Wortis (ed) *Mental Retardation and Developmental Disabilities*, Vol. 13 (London: Plenum Press).

Llewellyn, G. (1994) 'General Family Support Systems: are parents with learning disabilities catered for?' *Mental Handicap Research* 1, 21–8.

Machover, K. (1949) *Personality Projection in the Drawing of the Human Figure* (Springfield, Ill: Thomas).

Mannoni (1968) *The Child, His 'illness' and the Others*, trans (London: Penguin).

Markova, I., Jahoda, A., Cattermole, M. and Woodward, D. (1992) 'Living in hospital and Hostel: the pattern of interactions in people with learning disabilities', *Journal of Intellectual Disability Research* 36, 115–27.

Marks, D. (2000) *Disability: Controversial Debates and Psychosocial Perspectives* (London: Routledge).

Mattison, V. and Pistrang, N. (2000) *Saying Goodbye: When Keyworker Relationships End* (London: Free Association Press).

McCarthy, M. (2001) 'Women with Learning Disabilities – Experiencing their Sexuality in a Healthy Way', *Tizard Learning Disability Review* 6(1), 16–22.

McCarthy, M. and Thompson, D. (1997) 'A Prevalence Study of Sexual Abuse of Adults with Intellectual Disabilities Referred for Sex Education', *Journal of Applied Research in Intellectual Disabilities* 10, 105–24.

McCormack, B. (1991) 'Thinking, Discourse and the Denial of History: psychodynamic aspects of mental handicap', *Irish Journal of Psychological Medicine* 8, 59–64.

McDonnell, A. (1997) 'Training Care Staff to Manage Challenging Behaviour: an evaluation of a three-day training course', *British Journal of Developmental Disabilities* 43(2), 156–62.

McFadyen, A. (1998) 'Doubly Disadvantaged: providing a psychotherapeutic and educational service to children with complex disorders and their families', *Clinical Child Psychology and Psychiatry* 4(1), 91–105.

McGaw, S. and Sturmey, P. (1994) 'Assessing Parents with Learning Disabilities: The Parent Skills Model', *Child Abuse Review* 3, 1–14.

McLean, L.K. Brady, N.C. and McLean, J.E. (1996) 'Reported Communication Abilities of Individuals with Severe Mental Retardation', *American Journal on Mental Retardation* 100, 580–91.

Mental Deficiency Act (1913) (London: HMSO).

Menzies, I.E.P. (1959) 'The Functioning of Social Systems as a Defence against Anxiety', *Human Relations* 13, 95–121.

Meltzer, D. (1968) 'Terror, Persecution, Dread', *International Journal of Psychoanalysis* 49, 396–400.

Miller, L. and Rustin, M. (eds) (1989) *Closely Observed Infants* (London: Duckworth).

Miller, S.G. (1974) *An Exploratory Study of Sibling Relationships in Families with Retarded Children* (Doctoral dissertation, Columbia University, 1974) *Dissertation Abstracts International* 35, 2994B–2995B.

Mittler, P. and Sinason, V. (eds) (1996) *Changing Policy and Practice for People with Learning Disabilities* (London: Cassell Education).

Money-Kyrle, R. (1956) 'Normal Counter-Transference and Some of its Deviations', in (1978) *The Collected Papers of Roger Money-Kyrle* (Perth: Clunie).

Moss, S. (1995) 'Methodological Issues in the Diagnosis of Psychiatric Disorders in Adults with Learning Disability', *Thornfield Journal* 18, 9–18.

Moylan, D. (1994) 'The Dangers of Contagion: projective identification processes in institutions', in A. Obholzer and V. Zagier-Roberts (eds) *The unconscious at work: Individual and organisational stress in the human services* (London and New York: Routledge).

Nezu, C.M. and Nezu, A.M. (1994) 'Outpatient Psychotherapy for Adults with Mental Retardation and Concomitant Psychopathology: research and clinical imperatives', *Journal of Consulting and Clinical Psychology* 62, 34–42.

Obholzer, A. and Zagier Roberts, V. (1994) 'The Unconscious at Work: Individual and Organisational Stress', in *Human Services* (London: Routledge).

O'Brien, J. (1987) 'A Guide to Life Style Planning', in B.W. Wilcox and G.T. Bellamy (eds) *The Activities Catalogue: An alternative curriculum for youth and adults with severe disabilities* (Baltimore: Brookes).

O'Connor, H. (2001) 'Will We Grow Out of It? A psychotherapy group for people with learning disabilities', *Psychodynamic counselling* 7(3), 297–314.

Office of Population Censuses and Surveys (1989) The *Prevalence of Disability in Great Britain* (London: HMSO).

Orlinsky, D. and Howard, K. (1986) 'Process and Outcome in Psychotherapy', in S. Garfield and A. Bergin (eds) *Handbook of Psychotherapy and Behaviour Change* (London: Wiley).

Orlinsky, D.E., Grawe, K. and Parkes, B.K. (1994) 'Process and Outcome in Psychotherapy', in A.E. Bergin and S.L. Garfield (eds) *Handbook of Psychotherapy and Behavior Change* (New York: Wiley).

Oswin, M. (1981) *Am I Allowed to Cry? A Study of Bereavement Amongst People Who Have Learning Difficulties* (London: Human Horizons).

Oswin, M. (1985) 'Bereavement and Mental Handicap', in M. Craft, J. Bicknall and S. Hollins (eds) *Mental Handicap: A Multidisciplinary Approach* (Balliere Tindall).

Oxford English Dictionary (1997) (London: BAC).

Pantlin, A.W. (1985) 'Group Analytic Psychotherapy with Mentally Handicapped Patients', *Group Analysis* 18(1), 44–53.

Parkes, C.M. (1972) *Bereavement: Studies of Grief in Adult Life* (London: Penguin).

Parsons, J. and Upson, P. (1986) *Psychodynamic Psychotherapy with Mentally Handicapped Patients: Technical Issues*, Paper Presented at the Tavistock Clinic, Open Meeting.

Quigley, A., Murra, G., McKenzie, K. and Gordon, E. (2001) 'Staff Knowledge about Symptoms of Mental Health Problems in People with Learning Disabilities', *Journal of Learning Disabilities* Vol. 5(3), 235–44.

Powell, T. and Gallagher, P. (1993) *Brothers and Sisters: A Special Part of Exceptional Families.* (Baltimare: Paul H. Brookes).

Raphael-Leff, J. (1993) *Pregnancy: The Inside Story* (Sheldon Press).

Raynes, N., Pettipher, C., Shiell, A. and Wright, K. (1990) 'Keep Up the Small Talk', *Health Service Journal*, August, 1149.

Razza, N.J. (1993) 'Determinants of Direct Care Staff Turnover in Group Homes for Individuals with Mental Retardation', *Mental Retardation* 31, 284–91.

Reid, S. (1988) 'Interpretation: food for thought', Unpublished paper given to the study weekend of the Association of Child Psychotherapists.

Reid, S. (1997) 'The Development of Autistic Defences in an infant: the use of a single case study for research', *The International Journal of Infant Observation* (1)1, 51–71.

Reiss, S. (1995) 'Psychopathology in Mental Retardation', in N. Bouras (ed) (1994) *Mental Health in Mental Retardation: Recent advances and practices* (Cambridge: Cambridge University Press).

Richardson, A. and Ritchie, J. (1989) *Letting Go: dilemmas for parents whose son or daughter has a mental handicap* (London: Open University Press).

Robertson, J., Emerson, E., Gregory, N., Hatton, C., Kessissoglou, S., Hallam, A. and Linehan, C. (2001) 'Social Networks of People with Intellectual Disabilities in Residential Settings', *Mental Retardation* 39(3), 201–14.

Rose, J. (1993) 'Stress and Staff in Residential Settings: the move from hospital to the community', *Mental Handicap Research* 6(4), 312–32.

Rose, J. (1995) 'Stress and Residential Staff: towards an integration of existing research', *Mental Handicap Research* 8(4), 220–36.

Rosenburg, M. (1965) *Society and the Adolescent Self Esteem* (Princeton University Press).

Rustin, M. (1998) 'Dialogues with parents', *Journal of Child Psychotherapy* 24(2), 233–52.

Rycroft, C. (1972) *A Critical Dictionary of Psychoanalysis* (Harmondsworth: Penguin).

Ryle, A. (1975) *Frames and Cages: the repertory grid approach to human understanding* (London: Chatto and Windus).

Sant Angelo, D., Yerbury, A., Chalcroft, I., McVey, S. and Jenkins, C. (2001) 'Group Think: can group work with people with learning disabilities be an effective approach?' *Learning Disabilities Practice* 3(6), 26–8.

Schalock, R.L. (1996) *Quality of life: Volume 1 – Conceptualisation and Measurement* (Washington DC: American Association on Mental Retardation).

Schein, E.H. (1987) *Process Consultation* (Reading, M.A.: Addison-Wesley).

Seligman, M. and Darling, R.B. (1989) *Ordinary Families, Special Children: A systems approach to childhood disability* (London: The Guilford Press).

Seltzer, G.B., Begun, A., Seltzer, M.M. and Krauss, M.W. (1991) 'The Impacts of Siblings on Adults with Mental Retardation and their Aging Mothers', *Family Relations* 40, 310–17.

Sharrard, H. (1992) 'Feeling the strain: job stress and satisfaction of direct-care staff in the mental handicap service', *The British Journal of Mental Subnormality* 38(1), 32–8.

Sheppard, N. (1991) 'Quality of Life of People with Learning Disabilities: hospitals versus community homes', Unpublished Dissertation.

Sheppard, R. (1991) 'Sex Therapy and People with Learning Difficulties', *Sexual and Marital Therapy* 6(3), 307–16.

Sinason, V. (1990) 'Emotional Understanding', *Openmind* 45, 14.

Sinason, V. (1992) *Mental Handicap and the Human Condition: New Approaches from the Tavistock* (London: Free Association Books).

Sinason, V. (1999) 'The Psychotherapeutic Needs of the Learning Disabled and Multiply Disabled Child', in M. Lanyado and A. Horne *The Handbook of Child and Adolescent Psychotherapy* (London: Routledge).

Skene, R.A. (1991) 'Towards a Measure of Psychotherapy in Mental Handicap', *The British Journal of Mental Subnormality* 37(2), 101–10.

Smith, T., Parker, T., Taubman, M. and Lovass O.I. (1992) 'Transfer of Staff Training from Workshops to Group Homes: a failure to generalise across settings', *Research in Developmental Disabilities* 13(1), 57–71.

Stenfert-Kroese, B., Dagnan, D. and Loumidis, K. (1997) *Cognitive Behavioural Therapy for People with Learning Disabilities* (London Routledge).

Sternfert-Kroese, B. (2001) 'User's Survey of Parenting Services and the Use of Appropriate Psychological Measures', paper presented at 'Special Parenting' Back to Basics Conference, British Psychological Society – Special Interest Group – People with Learning Disabilities, April 2001.

Stern, D. (1985) *The Interpersonal World of the Infant* (New York: Basic Books).

Stern, D. (1995) *The Motherhood Constellation: a unified view of parent infant psychotherapy* (New York: Basic Books).

Stokes, J. (1987) 'Insights from Psychotherapy', paper presented at the International Symposium on Mental Handicap, Royal Society of Medicine, 25.2.1987.

Stokes, J. (1994) 'Problems in Multidisciplinary Teams: the unconscious at work', *Journal of Social Work Practice* 8(2), 161–7.

Strohmer, D.C. and Prout, H.T. (1994) *Counseling and Psychotherapy with*

Persons with Mental Retardation and Borderline Intelligence (Vermont: Clinical Psychology Publishing Company).

Symington, N. (1981) 'The Psychotherapy of a Subnormal Patient', *British Journal of Medical Psychology* 54, 187–99.

Symington, N. (1992) 'Countertransference with Mentally Handicapped Clients', in A. Waitman and S. Conboy-Hill (eds) *Psychotherapy and Mental Handicap* (London: Sage).

Szivos, S. and Griffiths, E. (1992) 'Coming to Terms with Learning Difficulties: the effects of group work and group processes on stigmatised identity', in A. Waitman and S. Conboy-Hill (eds) *Psychotherapy and Mental Handicap* (London: Sage).

Thomas, B. (2001) 'I've Taught You Once Already': forgetting the disability in learning disabilities', *Clinical Psychology Forum* 148, 26–8.

Todd, S. and Shearn, J. (1996) 'Struggles with Time: the careers of parents of adult sons and daughters with learning disabilities', *Disability and Society* 12(3), 341–66.

Trent, J.W. (1995) *Inventing the Feebleminded: A History of Mental Retardation in the United States* (Berkeley: University of California Press).

Trevarthen, C. (1976) 'Descriptive Analyses of Infant Communication Behaviour', in H.R. Schaffer (ed) *Studies in Mother-Interaction* (London: Academic Press).

Trowell, J. (1995) 'Organisations', in J. Trowell and M. Bower (eds) *The Emotional Needs of Young Children and Their Families: Using Psychoanalytic Ideas in the Community* (London: Routledge).

Tymchuk, A. (1991) 'Assessing Home Dangers and Safety Precautions: instruments for use', *Mental Handicap* 19, 4–10.

Tymchuk, A. and Andron, L. (1994) 'Rationale Approaches, Results and Resource Implications of Programmes to Enhance Parenting Skills in People with Learning Disabilities', in A. Craft (ed) *Practice Issues in Sexuality and Learning Disabilities* (London: Routledge).

Van der Gaag, A. (1998) 'Communication Skills and Adults with Learning Disabilities: eliminating professional myopia', *British Journal of Learning Disabilities* 26, 88–93.

Vetere, A. (1993) 'Using Family Therapy in Services for People with Learning disabilities', in J. Carpenter and A. Treacher (eds) *Using Family Therapy in the 90s* (Oxford: Blackwell).

Waitman, A. and Conboy-Hill, S. (eds) (1992) *Psychotherapy and Mental Handicap* (London: Sage).

Winnicott, D. (1949) *From Paediatrics to Psychoanalysis* (London: Hogarth).

Winnicott, D. (1962) *The Maturational Process and the Facilitating Environment* (London: Hogarth Press).

Wolfensberger, W. (1972) *The Principle of Normalisation in Human Services* Toronto: National Institute of Mental Retardation.

World Health Organisation (1992) *ICD-10 International Statistical Classification of Diseases and Related Health Problems*, 10th revision (Geneva: WHO).

Wright, D. (1996) ' "Childlike in his Innocence": lay attitudes to "idiots" and "imbeciles" in Victorian England', in D. Wright and A. Digby (eds)

From Idiocy to Mental Deficiency: Historical Perspectives on People with Learning Disabilities (London: Routledge).

Yalom, I.D. (1995) *The Theory and Practice of Group Psychotherapy* (4th edition) (Basic Books: New York).

Zagier-Roberts, V. (1998) 'When Dreams become Nightmares', in A. Foster and V. Zagier Roberts (eds) *Managing Mental Health in the Community Chaos and Containment* (London, New York: Routledge).

Zaharia, E.S. and Baumeister, A.A. (1979) 'Technician Losses in Public Residential Facilities', *American Journal of Mental Deficiency* 84, 36–9.

Zetlin, A.G. (1986) 'Mentally Retarded Adults and their Siblings', *American Journal of Mental Deficiency* 91(3), 217–25.

Guardian 19/05/2000 *'Appeal court bars sterilisation of woman with learning disabilities'*; Sunday Mail, 19/03/2000 *'Abigail is 13 and finding out about boys . . . now her mum wants her sterilised.'* Daily Telegraph, 27/01/2000 *'Handicapped woman to lose womb without consent'*; Guardian 24/11/1999 *'Court asked to order vasectomy on Down's syndrome man'*. (Department of Health, 2000).

INDEX